Kaplan Publishing are constantly finding new ways to make a difference to your studies and our exciting online resources really do offer something different to students looking for exam success.

This book comes with free MyKaplan online resources so that you can study anytime, anywhere

Having purchased this book, you have access to the following online study materials:

CONTENT	ACCA (including FFA,FAB,FMA)		AAT		FIA (excluding FFA,FAB,FMA)	
	Text	Kit	Text	Kit	Text	Kit
iPaper version of the book	✓	✓	✓	✓	✓	✓
Interactive electronic version of the book	✓					
Progress tests with instant answers	✓		✓			
Mock assessments online			✓	✓		
Material updates	✓	✓	✓	✓	✓	✓
Latest official ACCA exam questions		✓				
Extra question assistance using the signpost icon*		✓				
Timed questions with an online tutor debrief using the clock icon*		✓				
Interim assessment including questions and answers	✓				✓	
Technical articles	✓	✓			✓	✓

* Excludes F1, F2, F3, FFA, FAB, FMA

How to access your online resources

Kaplan Financial students will already have a MyKaplan account and these extra resources will be available to you online. You do not need to register again, as this process was completed when you enrolled. If you are having problems accessing online materials, please ask your course administrator.

If you are already a registered MyKaplan user go to www.MyKaplan.co.uk and log in. Select the 'add a book' feature and enter the ISBN number of this book and the unique pass key at the bottom of this card. Then click 'finished' or 'add another book'. You may add as many books as you have purchased from this screen.

If you purchased through Kaplan Flexible Learning or via the Kaplan Publishing website you will automatically receive an e-mail invitation to MyKaplan. Please register your details using this email to gain access to your content. If you do not receive the e-mail or book content, please contact Kaplan Flexible Learning.

If you are a new MyKaplan user register at www.MyKaplan.co.uk and click on the link contained in the email we sent you to activate your account. Then select the 'add a book' feature, enter the ISBN number of this book and the unique pass key at the bottom of this card. Then click 'finished' or 'add another book'.

Your Code and Information

This code can only be used once for the registration of one book online. This registration and your online content will expire when the final sittings for the examinations covered by this book have taken place. Please allow one hour from the time you submit your book details for us to process your request.

Please scratch the film to access your MyKaplan code.

Please be aware that this code is case-sensitive and you will need to include the dashes within the passcode, but not when entering the ISBN. For further technical support, please visit www.MyKaplan.co.uk

CREDIT CONTROL

Qualifications and Credit Framework

AQ2013 Level 4 Diploma in Accounting

British Library Cataloguing-in-Publication Data

A catalogue record for this book is available from the British Library.

Published by
Kaplan Publishing UK
Unit 2, The Business Centre
Molly Millars Lane
Wokingham
Berkshire
RG41 2QZ

ISBN 978 0 85732 948 6

We are grateful to the Association of Accounting Technicians for permission to reproduce past assessment materials and example tasks based on the new syllabus. The solutions to past answers and similar activities in the style of the new syllabus have been prepared by Kaplan Publishing.

CONTENTS

INTRODUCTION

HOW TO USE THESE MATERIALS

These Kaplan Publishing learning materials have been carefully designed to make your learning experience as easy as possible and to give you the best chance of success in your AAT assessments.

They contain a number of features to help you in the study process.

The sections on the Unit Guide, the Assessment and Study Skills should be read before you commence your studies.

They are designed to familiarise you with the nature and content of the assessment and to give you tips on how best to approach your studies.

STUDY TEXT

This study text has been specially prepared for the revised AAT qualification introduced in September 2013.

It is written in a practical and interactive style:

- key terms and concepts are clearly defined

- all topics are illustrated with practical examples with clearly worked solutions based on sample tasks provided by the AAT in the new examining style

- frequent activities throughout the chapters ensure that what you have learnt is regularly reinforced

- 'pitfalls' and 'examination tips' help you avoid commonly made mistakes and help you focus on what is required to perform well in your examination

- practice activities can be completed at the end of each chapter.

WORKBOOK

The workbook comprises:

Practice activities at the end of each chapter with solutions at the end of this text, to reinforce the work covered in each chapter.

The questions are divided into their relevant chapters and students may either attempt these questions as they work through the textbook, or leave some or all of these until they have completed the textbook as a final revision of what they have studied.

ICONS

The study chapters include the following icons throughout.

They are designed to assist you in your studies by identifying key definitions and the points at which you can test yourself on the knowledge gained.

Definition

These sections explain important areas of knowledge which must be understood and reproduced in an assessment.

Example

The illustrative examples can be used to help develop an understanding of topics before attempting the activity exercises.

Activity

These are exercises which give the opportunity to assess your understanding of all the assessment areas.

Quality and accuracy are of the upmost importance to us so if you spot an error in any of our products, please send an email to mykaplanreporting@kaplan.com with full details, or follow the link to the feedback form in MyKaplan.

Our Quality Co-ordinator will work with our technical team to verify the error and take action to ensure it is corrected in future editions.

UNIT GUIDE

Credit Control covers both knowledge and skills.

Principles of Credit Management (Knowledge)

2 credits

Control of Debt and Credit (Skills)

3 credits

Purpose of the unit

This unit is about understanding, applying and demonstrating the principles of credit control in managing the granting of credit and collection of amounts outstanding from customers in an organisation. The learner will be able to give advice on the granting of credit, and also the collection of monies owed in compliance with relevant legislation, good practice and organisational policy.

The student must understand the basics of contract law and the Data Protection Act and have knowledge of procedures for assessing credit and managing the collection of amounts outstanding. They must also have a detailed understanding of the actions available to aid the collection of receivables, types of insolvency situations and the implication insolvency may have on the actions which can be taken.

Successful students will be able to grant credit to customers by following good practice, reviewing customer information, considering a range of factors having particular regard to organisational guidelines. Students need to be able to select and use a range of tools when granting credit. Assessment tasks will feature questions where the organisation has strict guidelines such as a credit rating scoring system whilst other questions may involve a subjective assessment of credit worthiness by calculating and interpreting key ratios. This is a key topic area which will be assessed and students must ensure that they have a thorough understanding of the calculations and be able to interpret those calculations. Students also need to understand the interrelationship between the ratios. Students will be required to evaluate the current credit status of existing customers and potential customers.

Learning objectives

On completion of this unit the learner will be able to:

- Understand relevant legislation that impacts upon credit management.
- Use information from a variety of sources to grant credit to customers within organisational guidelines.
- Use a range of techniques for the collection of debts.
- Monitor and control the supply of credit.

Learning Outcomes and Assessment criteria

The unit consists of four learning outcomes which are further broken down into assessment criteria. These are set out in the following table with learning outcomes in bold type and Assessment criteria listed underneath each learning outcome. A K indicates a knowledge criteria and an S indicates a skill criteria. Reference is also made to the relevant chapter within the text.

To perform this unit effectively you will need to know and understand the following:

		Chapter
1	**Understand relevant legislation that impacts upon credit management**	
1.1K	Explain how the main features of contract law are applied in relation to the credit an organisation offers its customers	1
1.2K	Describe remedies for breach of contract	1
1.3K	Define the terms and conditions associated with contracts relating to the granting of credit	1
1.4K	Explain the importance of data protection legislation and its application to credit management	1
2	**Use information from a variety of sources to grant credit to customers within organisational guidelines**	
2.1K	Identify sources of credit status and related information used to assess the risk of granting credit	2

KAPLAN PUBLISHING

Delivery guidance

The AAT have provided delivery guidance giving further details of the way in which the unit will be assessed.

1   Understand relevant legislation that impacts upon credit management

Students will need to demonstrate that they understand how legislation impacts upon the credit control function. Whilst the credit controller does not need to be a qualified lawyer, there is some basic legislation which students need to understand and be able to define and explain.

1.1K Explain how the main features of contract law are applied in relation to the credit an organisation offers its customers

In order to ensure that money is received for the sale of goods or the provision of services the credit controller needs to be able to explain the main features of contract law, which include offer and acceptance, remedies available in order to collect outstanding amounts, which include an action for price, and remedies available in the case of customer insolvency, which include retention of title claims.

The legislation that impacts upon credit control includes contract law. Students need to have knowledge, understanding, and be able to define and explain the essential characteristics of a contract (including invitation to treat, offer, consideration, intention to create legal relations and acceptance).

Students need to distinguish between documents which form the contract (written order from a customer) and those which are simply an invitation to treat (trade price list). Students will be given various scenarios and have to decide the position of the scenario and the contract law implications. For example, if Bob places a note in the rear window of his car stating 'For sale £300' the note is an example of what? Answer – An invitation to treat.

Other relevant legislation

Trade Descriptions Act – students need to understand that it is a criminal offence to make a false statement or to make a misleading statement. Students may have to comment on whether a scenario is in breach of this act.

Unfair Contract Terms Act – students need to understand that unfair terms cannot be part of a contract.

KAPLAN PUBLISHING

Sale of Goods Act 1979 – students need to understand when the Sale of Goods Act applies, when title to the goods pass, what conditions can be attached and the key terms of 'satisfactory quality', 'fit for purpose', 'as described'.

Consumer Credit Act 1974 – students need to understand the key terms of the act.

1.2K Describe remedies for breach of contract

Students need to understand and be able to describe and explain the main remedies for breach of contract including damages and specific performance and the Late Payment of Commercial Debts (Interest) Act 1998.

Late Payment of Commercial Debts (Interest) Act 1998

Students may be required to calculate the late payment interest for a given outstanding amount and a given Bank of England (BoE) base rate. Students need to know that the interest rate is 8% above the Bank of England base rate for the period the debt is late, the interest is based upon the VAT inclusive amount and calculated as a simple interest rate. For example if the debt is £4,000 plus VAT, BoE rate is 1% and the debt is 40 days late the calculation is £4,000 × 1.2 × 0.09 × 40/365.

1.3K Define the terms and conditions associated with contracts relating to the grant of credit

Students need to be able to define the terms and conditions associated with contracts including offer, acceptance, intention to create legal relations, consideration, capacity to create a contract, consent to the terms, legal and possible, void contracts, voidable contracts, unenforceable contracts and retention of title clauses.

1.4K Explain the importance of data protection legislation and its application to credit management

Students need to be able to explain the importance of data protection legislation and how it affects both company and individual customers. Students need to understand that the Data Protection Act applies to individuals and not companies. Students need to be able to explain how the act applies to credit management; for example, the security and use of data.

2 Use information from a variety of sources to grant credit to customers within organisational guidelines

Students will need to demonstrate that they understand how to prepare and use information from various sources to manage the granting of credit. The information used to assess credit can be either externally generated or internally generated. The main types of externally generated information are: trade credit references, bank references, credit reference agency reports, statutory accounts, management accounts provided by the customer. The main types of internally generated information include trading history (for existing customers), information from the sales department, and reports generated from external information such as ratio calculations.

Students need to have an understanding of why this information is needed and explain how to use it. Students may be required to explain the usefulness of various types of information and explain how to select the most appropriate type to use in a given scenario. This learning outcome may also be assessed indirectly by requiring students to apply their understanding to a given scenario and recommend a course of action.

Key to the management of credit is the information available for the assessment of whether to grant credit in the first place. There is often a large range of data available and it is important to know the types of data, how it can be used, and the integrity of the data.

2.1K Identify sources of credit status and related information used to assess the risk of granting credit

Students will need to be familiar with the types and structure of credit information. Students may be required to explain and describe the most appropriate type of information to be used in a particular case and explain how the information can be used in order to decide whether or not credit should be given. Below is the list of information which students need to be able to identify, describe and explain:

- credit rating agencies reports
- supplier references
- bank references
- statutory accounts (filed at Companies House)
- management accounts (if available)
- information provided by colleagues
- official publications.

2.2K Explain methods of assessing credit control information

Students need to be able to explain the following methods of analysing credit control information:

- Age analysis – an explanation of what an age analysis is, the importance of an accurate and timely age analysis, how to use an aged analysis and why it is needed in order to efficiently manage credit.

- Average periods of credit given and received – an explanation of what is an average period of credit and how a rapidly expanding revenue can affect the measure of the average period of credit.

- Incidence of irrecoverable and doubtful debts – an explanation of an irrecoverable debt and a doubtful debt and how each affects the cash flow of the organisation.

Students may be required to prepare extracts from an aged receivables report by taking opening balances and adjusting for invoices, receipts, credit notes and a restocking fee.

2.3S Assess the current credit status of customers and potential customers

This is one of the key topic areas which will be assessed and students must ensure that they have a thorough understanding of the calculations and interpretation of the calculations. Students also need to understand the interrelationship between the ratios. Students will be required to evaluate the current credit status of existing customers and potential customers. This process will be undertaken by using a variety of information collected from both internal and external sources. The information which may be provided for evaluation includes the following:

- credit rating agencies reports
- supplier references
- bank references
- statutory accounts filed at companies house
- management accounts
- credit circle reports
- information provided by colleagues
- official publications

Students will be required to extract relevant information and possibly prepare calculations based upon the information provided. Students will be required to prepare ratio calculations based upon published financial information and management accounting information.

Students may be required to explain and use ratios to evaluate credit status. Students may also be required to use a credit scoring system where they have to calculate a credit score based upon a range of performance indicators.

Students may be required to assess financial information and comment on the risk of overtrading or conclude whether the organisation is overtrading by considering key indicators of overtrading and suggesting how to manage overtrading.

The following financial performance indicators may be assessed:

- Liquidity indicators

    - Current ratio – current assets/current liabilities can be shown as X:1 or simply X. In computer based tasks please show as X. For example if the current assets are £10,000 and the current liabilities are £8,000 show the ratio as 10/8 = 1.25.

    - Quick ratio – current assets less inventory/current liabilities again shown a X:1 or X. In computer based assessments show as X.

    - Accounts receivable collection period – Trade receivables/Sales revenue × 365.

    - Accounts payable payment period – Trade payables/Cost of sales × 365.

    - Inventory holding period in days – Inventory/Cost of sales × 365.

- Profitability indicators

    - Gross profit margin= Gross profit/Sales revenue × 100%

    - Profit for the period margin = Profit/Sales revenue × 100%

    - Interest cover = Profit/Interest payable shown as a number

    - Return on Net assets = Profit/Capital employed or net assets

- Debt indicators

    - Gearing ratio – The gearing ratio can be calculated as either Total debt/(Total debt plus equity) × 100% or Total debt/Total equity × 100%. Total debt must include both long term and short term debt. Both computer marked and human marked tasks will allow both calculations.

    - Short term debt ratio – short term debt as a percentage of total debt.

- Cash flow indicators

    – EBITDA – earnings before interest, tax, depreciation and amortisation.

    – EBITDA interest cover – EBITDA/finance costs (statement of profit or loss (income statement)) or EBITDA/interest paid (cash flow statement, if available).

    – EBITDA to total debt.

2.4S Agree credit terms with new customers or changes to credit terms with existing customers

Once the customer's information has been assessed, credit terms can be agreed. Students may be given the organisation's policy and required to set appropriate terms. This may include size of any credit limit and terms of payment of invoices as well as terms such as retention of title. Students may be required to decide on the size of a credit limit based upon the expected orders notified by the sales department. For example, a new customer may have passed the evaluation stage and the sales department expects to receive weekly orders of £5,000. Clearly a credit limit of £10,000 will not be sufficient.

Credit insurance may be used and this may inform the decision as to whether to agree credit and set appropriate levels. Students need to understand credit insurance and may be required to explain a given credit insurance opinion. Students may also be required to advise management on whether to trade with a new customer where credit insurance has been refused.

Students may be required to agree changes to current levels of credit in response from a request from a customer or salesman. Examinations may provide additional information and require students to assess whether the credit levels or terms should be changed. For example, a new customer may be given a £10,000 credit limit and after trading for several months place an order for £15,000. The decision will depend on an assessment to include the trading history of the customer and whether they have kept within their current limit and paid to terms.

2.5S Communicate tactfully the reasons for refusing or extending credit with customers

Students may be required to draft a response to a customer's request for credit where this request has been refused. Students may be required to explain how the refusal of credit should be made and what should be included in a refusal. The refusal should be polite, explain the reasons for refusal, and explain what the company could do to improve their chances of obtaining credit in future including trading on a cash basis to establish a trading history.

3 Use a range of techniques for the collection of debts

Students will need to be aware of credit control processes and the techniques and methods that may be used to efficiently collect outstanding customer accounts. Students may be required to explain how to communicate with customers, when to communicate with customers, when to instruct a debt collection agency, when to instruct solicitors and when to issue proceedings.

Students need to be aware that there is a range of techniques and methods for the collection of outstanding monies. These include the correct application of contract law, various ways to communicate with the customer and various time frames for this communication. The type of communication will depend on the nature of the goods or services. It is unlikely that a stationery company will meet face to face to discuss payment terms, whereas a defence contractor with a multi-million-pound order is likely to have detailed face-to-face meetings to agree prices and payment schedules, probably with interim payments during the contract.

3.1K Explain legal and administrative procedures for the collection of debts

Students need to be able to explain the administrative process for the collection of outstanding accounts. This process starts with the receipt of an order and finishes with the posting of the cash received from the customer. Students need to be able to explain the stages in the process and explain the importance of each stage and how earlier stages such as establishing the contract are fundamental to ensuring that customers pay on time, or that action can be taken which will result in the successful collection of a debt.

Students need to know the legal and administrative procedures which must be followed for collecting amounts outstanding from customers. Outstanding amounts owed to an entity are civil claims. Those with a value under £5,000 will be dealt with in the County Court under the Small Claims Track (sometimes known to the lay public as 'Small Claims Court', although it is not a separate court). Claims between £5,000 and £25,000 that are capable of being tried within one day are allocated to the 'Fast Track' and claims over £25,000 or complex cases where the amount is less than £25,000 but will require more than one day in court are allocated to the 'Multi Track' route. These 'tracks' are labels for the use of the court system not separate courts. A judge will decide if the case will be dealt with in a 'fast track' or 'multi-track' hearing once initial paperwork has been filed by the claimant and the defendant.

Students also need to know ways of enforcing a judgement which include – garnishee order, warrant of execution, warrant of delivery, attachment of earnings, charging order

1   the role of the debt collection agency.

2   the role of solicitors.

3.2K Evaluate a range of methods for the collection and management of debts

Students need to be able to identify methods for the collection and management of debts and explain the appropriateness of each method. These methods include:

- clear credit control policy

- written communication (the sending of invoices, statements, solicitors letters)

- the use of telecommunications (contact via the telephone, email, internet)

- restricting future trade (placing on stop), reducing credit limits, reducing payment terms.

- the use of third parties such as debt collection agencies, factoring companies, credit insurance companies, solicitors

- small claims summons, County Court summons, High Court summons

- the use of the Late Payment of Commercial Debts (Interest) Act 1998.

3.3S Select debt recovery methods appropriate to individual outstanding receivables

Students may be given an aged trade receivables report which requires analysis and recommended actions. Students need to be able to consider the aged trade receivable analysis and supplementary information in order to select an appropriate recovery method. Methods include a telephone call, letter or statement, use of a debt collection agency, legal proceedings or possible negotiating with an insolvent company or insolvency practitioner. Students may also have to evaluate retention of title claims and suggest action to invoke retention of title (ROT).

3.4S Explain the reasons for offering discounts for prompt payment and the effects on the organisation of offering such a discount

Students need to explain how offering discounts aids the liquidity of the organisation and explain how discounts can improve cash flow of the organisation. Students need also to be able to explain the cost of offering discounts and identify the effects. Students need to be able to calculate the annual equivalent cost of offering a discount under both a simple interest rate and the compound interest rate.

For example – Alpha offers a discount of 5% for payment within 14 days where the normal payment terms are 30 days. Calculate the annual equivalent interest rate (AEIR) ignoring compounding. The answer will be $5/95 \times 365/(30 - 14) = 1.2$ or 120%. Taking account of compounding results in a higher AEIR of $(1 + 5/95)$ to the power of $(365/(30 - 14))$ less 1 gives 2.22 which is 222%.

Students will require a scientific calculator in order to apply compounding.

4   Monitor and control the supply of credit

4.1K Explain the importance of liquidity management

Students need to be able to explain the importance of liquidity management and how an effective credit control function is fundamental to the liquidity of the business. For most businesses all their revenue is made on credit terms and therefore it is critical to manage the process in order to ensure that sales are only made to organisations which, it has been assessed, will pay to terms and that timely collection of these amounts is taken.

- Students need to be able to explain the importance of liquidity management and how an effective credit control function is fundamental to the liquidity of the business.

- Students need to be able to explain the difference between a cash sale and a credit sale and the risks associated with a credit sale.

- Students need to be able to explain the effect that increasing credit terms has on the cash flow of the business.

- Students may be required to explain the cost to the business of extending credit terms or giving cash discounts for prompt payment and its impact on liquidity management.

- Students need to be able to describe the main features of invoice discounting and factoring and explain how they can aid the liquidity management of the business. Credit insurance may be required as part of a factoring arrangement or may simply be another tool to aid liquidity management. Students may be required to explain the main features of credit insurance, how it aids credit control and its limitations.

- Students may be required to perform simple calculations relating to the amount of finance available under a factoring or invoice discounting facility or the cover available under a credit insurance facility.

4.2K Explain the effect on organisations following bankruptcy or insolvency of credit customers

Students need to be able to explain how the bankruptcy or insolvency of a customer may impact on the organisation. Students need to understand that supplying goods or services to a customer is an unsecured debt and that in the event of the insolvency of a customer, often little or no money will be received in lieu of the amount outstanding. Students need to be able to explain the types of personal insolvency and company insolvency and what action can be taken. This action could be invoking a retention of title clause in a contract, registering the debt with the insolvency practitioner and claiming relief for irrecoverable debts from HMRC to recover the VAT paid by the supplier to HMRC. Students need to know the differences between liquidation, administrative receivership, administration and personal bankruptcy.

4.3S Regularly analyse information relating to receivables' accounts

Students need to be able to identify a range of methods of analysing information on debtors including:

- aged analysis
- trading history
- average periods of credit
- 80/20 rule
- materiality
- status reports.

Students may be required to prepare ledger balances for individual customers by taking opening balances and adjusting for sales invoices, sales receipts, credit notes and restocking fees. Students will need to take account of VAT when dealing with these transactions.

4.4S Negotiate the payment of outstanding debts in a courteous and professional manner and record the outcome

Students may be required to prepare a telephone brief or letter which outlines the discussions/negotiations which have been entered into with a customer. For example, a customer may owe an amount of money and is offering to pay by instalments. It may have been decided by the credit controller that the customer will be allowed to pay over three or four instalments and that legal proceedings will not be entered into unless the instalments are not paid.

4.5S Promptly send information regarding significant outstanding amounts and potential irrecoverable debts to relevant individuals within the organisation

Students may be required to prepare an email/memo in response to a specific request, or as part of the monitoring of trade receivables, regarding significant outstanding amounts and suggest actions to taken and provisions to be made. This could include the suggestion to place an account on hold, instruct a debt collection agency or issue legal proceedings and to make a provision.

4.6S Make recommendations to write off irrecoverable debts and make provisions for doubtful debts based upon a realistic analysis of all known factors

Students will be required to recommend which outstanding amounts should be written off and provisions that should be made.

KAPLAN PUBLISHING

THE ASSESSMENT

The format of the assessment

The assessment is divided into seven standalone tasks which cover all of the learning outcomes and assessment criteria. Two of the tasks will require free text responses and will be human marked. The remaining five tasks will be computer marked.

Task	Learning outcome	Assessment criteria	Maximum marks	Title for topics with task range
1	1	1.1K 1.2K 1.3K 1.4K	20	Contract law – features, application and remedies. Data Protection Act
2	2, 3 and 4	2.1K 2.2K 3.1K 3.2K 3.4S 4.1K 4.2K	20	Procedures for granting credit and collection of debts
3	2	2.3S 2.4S 2.5S	24	Credit limit assessment using a rating system
4	2	2.3S 2.4S 2.5S	24	Credit limit assessment – calculation of ratios and evaluation
5	2	2.3S 2.4S 2.5S	24	Credit limit assessment analysis
6	3, 4	3.3S 4.3S 4.4S 4.5S 4.6S	18	Credit collection selection of action
7	3, 4	3.3S 4.3S 4.4S 4.5S 4.6S	18	Credit collection analysis and suggested action

Time allowed

The time allowed for this assessment is **2 hours 30 minutes.**

STUDY SKILLS

Preparing to study

Devise a study plan

Determine which times of the week you will study.

Split these times into sessions of at least one hour for study of new material. Any shorter periods could be used for revision or practice.

Put the times you plan to study onto a study plan for the weeks from now until the assessment and set yourself targets for each period of study – in your sessions make sure you cover the whole course, activities and the associated questions in the workbook at the back of the manual.

If you are studying more than one unit at a time, try to vary your subjects as this can help to keep you interested and see subjects as part of wider knowledge.

When working through your course, compare your progress with your plan and, if necessary, re-plan your work (perhaps including extra sessions) or, if you are ahead, do some extra revision/practice questions.

Effective studying

Active reading

You are not expected to learn the text by rote, rather, you must understand what you are reading and be able to use it to pass the assessment and develop good practice.

A good technique is to use SQ3Rs – Survey, Question, Read, Recall, Review:

1   **Survey the chapter**

     Look at the headings and read the introduction, knowledge, skills and content, so as to get an overview of what the chapter deals with.

2   **Question**

     Whilst undertaking the survey ask yourself the questions you hope the chapter will answer for you.

3 **Read**

Read through the chapter thoroughly working through the activities and, at the end, making sure that you can meet the learning objectives highlighted on the first page.

4 **Recall**

At the end of each section and at the end of the chapter, try to recall the main ideas of the section/chapter without referring to the text. This is best done after short break of a couple of minutes after the reading stage.

5 **Review**

Check that your recall notes are correct.

You may also find it helpful to re-read the chapter to try and see the topic(s) it deals with as a whole.

Note taking

Taking notes is a useful way of learning, but do not simply copy out the text.

The notes must:

* be in your own words
* be concise
* cover the key points
* well organised
* be modified as you study further chapters in this text or in related ones.

Trying to summarise a chapter without referring to the text can be a useful way of determining which areas you know and which you don't.

Three ways of taking notes

1 **Summarise the key points of a chapter**

2 **Make linear notes**

A list of headings, subdivided with sub-headings listing the key points.

If you use linear notes, you can use different colours to highlight key points and keep topic areas together.

Use plenty of space to make your notes easy to use.

3 **Try a diagrammatic form**

The most common of which is a mind map.

To make a mind map, put the main heading in the centre of the paper and put a circle around it.

Draw lines radiating from this to the main sub-headings which again have circles around them.

Continue the process from the sub-headings to sub-sub-headings.

Highlighting and underlining

You may find it useful to underline or highlight key points in your study text – but do be selective.

You may also wish to make notes in the margins.

Revision phase

Kaplan has produced material specifically designed for your final examination preparation for this unit.

These include pocket revision notes and a bank of revision questions specifically in the style of the new syllabus.

Further guidance on how to approach the final stage of your studies is given in these materials.

Further reading

In addition to this text, you should also read the 'Student section' of the 'Accounting Technician' magazine every month to keep abreast of any guidance from the examiners.

TERMINOLOGY FOR CRDC

There are different terms used to mean the same thing – you will need to be aware of both sets of terminology.

UK GAAP	IAS
Final accounts	Financial statements
Trading and profit and loss account	Statement of profit or loss
Turnover or sales	Revenue or Sales revenue
Balance sheet	Statement of financial position
Fixed assets	Non-current assets
Net book value	Carrying amount
Tangible assets	Property, plant and equipment
Stock	Inventory
Trade debtors	Trade receivables
Trade creditors	Trade payables
Long term liabilities	Non-current liabilities
Capital	Equity
Profit and loss balance	Retained earnings
Net profit	Profit for the year

Legislation

1

Introduction

This chapter covers the legislation that affects granting credit to customers, the characteristics of a contract, remedies for breaches of contract and other relevant legislation.

ASSESSMENT CRITERIA	CONTENTS
Explain how the main features of contract law are applied in relation to the credit the organisation offers its customers (1.1K)	1 Contract law
	2 Terms and conditions of contracts
Describe remedies for breach of contract (1.2K)	3 Remedies for breach of contract
Define the terms and conditions associated with contracts relating to the granting of credit (1.3K)	4 Data Protection Act
	5 Other legislation
Explain the importance of data protection legislation and its application to credit management (1.4K)	

1 Contract law

1.1 Introduction

Control of the credit given to a customer is important for any company. Most companies therefore appoint a **credit controller** whose responsibility it is to give appropriate credit terms to customers and ensure these terms are kept. **Receivables** are an important part of **working capital** and **careful management** of this asset is required to maintain the company's **liquidity**.

Credit controllers do not need to be qualified lawyers but it is important to understand the legal background to contracts and credit arrangements.

1.2 Nature of a contract

The sale of goods and services is a type of contract and therefore the credit controller must ensure that each party abides by this contract.

> **Definition**
>
> A **contract** is a legally binding agreement between two parties.

> **Definition**
>
> The **offeror** is the party making the offer.

> **Definition**
>
> The **offeree** is the party accepting the offer.

The **law of contract** is the branch of the civil law which determines whether or not a promise is legally binding (i.e. enforceable by a court of law).

1.3 The essential characteristics of a contract

There are certain requirements if a contract is to be valid:

- **offer** and **acceptance** (i.e. an agreement)

- the **intention to create legal relations** (i.e. the parties must be willing to submit to the authority of the law and be bound by their contracts)

- **consideration**, in that both parties must do, or promise to do, something as their side of the contract

- the parties must have the **capacity**, or ability, **to contract and submit** themselves to the authority of the law (children and mentally disordered people are restricted)

- the parties must genuinely **consent to the terms** of the contract in that they must not have been mistaken by the contract terms, or lied to in negotiations – there must be **certainty of terms**

- the contract itself must be both **legal** and **possible**

- **written formalities** may be observed in **some** situations.

The key factors are a basic understanding of offer, acceptance and consideration which will be detailed below.

1.4 Offer and acceptance

It is important to distinguish between an **offer** and an **invitation to treat**.

> **Q Definition**
>
> An **offer** is a definite and unequivocal statement of willingness to be bound on specified terms without further negotiations.

If you make an 'offer' it means that you are stating that you are willing to be bound to a contract in its current form with no changes required.

An offer can be in any form – oral, written or by conduct. However, it is not effective until it has been communicated to the offeree. For example, if a reward is offered for the return of a lost item, it cannot be claimed by someone who did not know of the reward before they returned the item.

> **Q Definition**
>
> An **invitation to treat** is not an offer. An invitation to treat means an invitation to the other party to make an offer.

An example of an **invitation to treat** is an advertisement, price ticket or trade price list where a written order from a customer is then the **offer.**

Once an offer has been made the next stage is for the contract to be accepted.

🔍 Definition

Acceptance is the unqualified and unconditional agreement to all the terms of the offer.

To be effective, the acceptance must be made while the offer is still in force; it must be **absolute**, **unqualified** and **communicated** to the offeror by word or action.

Offer and acceptance constitute agreement.

💡 Example

Joseph has a sign in his car stating 'For sale, £1,200'.

Benjamin sees the invitation to treat and offers £800 to Joseph.

Joseph does not accept but responds to Benjamin that the lowest he would accept is £1,000.

Benjamin accepts so long as the car has a valid MOT certificate.

This is still not an agreement as Benjamin's response has a criterion that must be met.

Once Joseph proves he has a valid MOT and Benjamin accepts this certificate there has been:

- an invitation to treat (sign in the car)
- an offer (to buy/sell the car) and
- acceptance (Benjamin approves of the certificate).

Therefore an agreement has been formed.

Termination of an offer

An offer can be terminated by:

- **Revocation** – an offer can be revoked by the offeror at any time before acceptance, even if the offeror has agreed to keep the offer open. The revocation must be communicated to the offeree, i.e. it must be brought to his actual notice. The revocation can be communicated by the offeror or a reliable third party. There are two exceptions to the above rules on revocation:

- If the offeree pays the offeror to keep the offer open, any revocation will amount to a breach of that contract. The offeree could claim damages for the loss of the opportunity to accept the offer, although he could not accept the offer itself.

- The offeror cannot revoke his offer once the offeree has begun to perform the acts which would amount to acceptance, for example if part payment has been made.

- **Rejection** – the offeree may reject the offer outright or may make a counter offer. A counter offer is an offer made in response to an offer. A request for further details does not constitute a counteroffer.

- **Lapse** – an offer will lapse on:
  - the death of the offeror (unless the offeree accepts in ignorance of the death)
  - the death of the offeree
  - after the expiry of a fixed time (if any) or after a reasonable time. What is a reasonable time may depend on the subject matter of the contract; if the goods are perishable the time for lapse will be very short.

Once an offer has been terminated, it cannot be accepted.

1.5   Consideration

Before a simple binding contract exists, both parties must have **agreed to provide something of value to the other**. The price which each has to pay is termed the consideration and converts the mere promises of the parties into bargains **enforceable by the courts**.

Q Definition

Consideration can be defined as 'some right, interest, profit or benefit accruing to one party, or some forbearance, detriment, loss or responsibility given, suffered or undertaken by the other'.

◌ Example

Joseph is selling his car and has agreed to sell it for £1,000 to Benjamin.

Joseph will be suffering the loss of his car but the benefit of gaining £1,000.

Benjamin will be suffering the loss of £1,000 but the benefit of gaining the car.

When deciding on what the consideration will be, the following should be observed:

- **Sufficient** – it must be of some value (an item or service), even if it is minimal value (**peppercorn**). The consideration is usually of monetary value. Another legal term used here is '**adequate'**, this means fair price. Consideration does not need to be adequate, but needs to be **sufficient** to form a contract.

- **Legal** – i.e. not against the law.

- **Should not be a duty which exists currently** - for example 'I will pay you £50 for not breaking the speed limit'. The speed limit is a legal requirement and is therefore a duty that already exists.

Consideration must be **executory** or **executed**, but **not past**:

- **Executory** – a promise to do something in the future is given in exchange for another promise to be done in the future. (I will pay you £10 if you get an A grade in your exam).

- **Executed** – a promise is actually executed, in exchange for another promise to be executed in the future. (I will pay you £5 now for you to wash my car at the weekend).

- **Past** – a promise has been given or executed before and independently of the other promise.

⦿ Example

Joseph offers to sell his car to Benjamin for £1,000. Benjamin agrees to pay £1,000 for Joseph's car. There has been offer and acceptance and consideration – a simple contract has been formed.

1.6   Intention to create legal relations

If an offer is accepted, then an agreement is created, but this agreement does not automatically become a contract. If one of the parties wishes to invoke the aid of the law in enforcing the terms of the agreement against the other party, he must show that there had been an intention by both parties that the agreement was to create legal relations.

There is a presumption in social or domestic agreements that legal relations are not intended. But in **commercial agreements**, it is generally **assumed that relations** are intended unless there is a clause in the agreement to the contrary.

Activity 1

Which of the following are features of a simple contract:

(i)   Offer

(ii)   Consideration

(iii)   Relations

(iv)   Acceptance

(v)   Invitation

(vi)   Certainty of terms

(vii)   Intention to create legal relations

A   All of them

B   (i), (ii), (iii), (v), (vi) only

C   (i), (ii), (iii), (iv) only

D   (i), (ii), (iv), (vi) and (vii)

Activity 2

Raphael has a notice in his shop window saying that the books he has for sale are half price. This is an example of:

A   Offer

B   Acceptance

C   Invitation to treat

D   Consideration

Activity 3

Barry is ordering an Indian takeaway on the telephone and says he will pay when he picks up the order. Which of the following would constitute consideration?

A   Placing the order

B   Paying for the order

C   Saying he will pay for the order

D   Picking up the order

Activity 4

Betty is the owner of a haberdashery and put a notice in the window of her shop advertising that all fabric has 20% off. This is:

A   A completed contract

B   An acceptance of an offer

C   A contractual offer

D   An invitation to treat

Activity 5

If you are shopping in a supermarket a contract is formed?

A   When you put your goods in the trolley

B   When you take items off the shelves

C   When the checkout assistant takes your goods

D   When you pay for the goods

2   Terms and conditions of contracts

2.1   Types of contracts

A **void** contract is one that **cannot be enforced by law**. An agreement to carry out an illegal act or an agreement that is impossible to carry out are examples of void contracts.

A **voidable** contract is a valid contract that **can be nullified** – one party is bound to a contract but the other party is not, so can withdraw from the contract. If this happens then the contract becomes void. A contract between an adult and a minor is an example of a voidable contract as the adult is bound by the contract but the minor is not as they are not of legal age.

An **unenforceable contract** is one that is **valid** (i.e. meets all the requirements listed above) but **if one party withdraws** from the contract the **courts of law will not enforce** them to meet the requirements of the contract.

A **frustrated contract** occurs if an unforeseen event either renders contractual obligations impossible, or radically changes the party's principal purpose for entering into the contract.

Frustrated contracts could occur in the following circumstances:

- An item or building essential to the contract is destroyed, through no fault of either party.

- A law is passed subsequent to the formation of the contract, which makes the contract illegal.

- A person or group under contract becomes unavailable through death, illness or unavailability (generally only applies for the performance of personal services and not for generic commercial services such as building work, which could be performed by numerous individuals).

An important limitation is that economic hardship, or a 'bad bargain', will not render a contract frustrated.

Activity 6

A void contract is a contract that:

A   Is valid

B   Can be enforced by the law

C   Can be nullified

D   Cannot be enforced by the law

2.2   Contractual terms

A statement, written or oral, made during the negotiations leading to a contract, may be a **term** of the contract or merely a **representation** inducing the contract.

A **representation** is something that is said by the offeror in order to persuade the offeree to enter into the contract. It may or may not become a term of that contract.

The distinction between terms and representations is important because, if a statement is untrue, the remedies available to the innocent party differ:

- if the representation becomes a term of the contract, the innocent party has remedies for breach of the term as well as for misrepresentation

- if, however, the representation does not become a term of the contract, the innocent party will have remedies only for misrepresentation which are based on equitable remedies.

2.3 Sources of terms

Terms may be **express** or **implied**.

Express terms are those specifically inserted into the contract by one or both of the parties. They must be clear for them to be enforceable.

Implied terms are not expressly included in the contract, but they are nevertheless still part of the contract. They may be implied by statute or by the courts.

Express terms will generally override implied terms. However, some statutory terms cannot be overridden by express agreement (for example, terms inserted by the Sale of Goods Act 1979).

There are three types of terms:

- A **condition** – is an important term going to the root of the contract. Breach can result in damages or discharge or both. Discharge entitles the innocent party to reject the contract and claim damages.

- A **warranty** – is a less important term, which is incidental to the main purpose of the contract. Breach of warranty results in damages only.

- An **innominate** or indeterminate term – is neither a condition nor a warranty. The remedy depends on the effects of the breach:

    - if trivial then damages only i.e. term is treated as if it were a warranty.

    - if serious then damages, discharge or both i.e. term is treated as if it were a condition.

3 Remedies for breach of contract

3.1 Introduction

Legal action can be taken to enforce a contract or to act as a remedy if a contract is breached. There are two types of **breach of contract**:

- **Actual** breach – when one party refuses or fails to complete the contract by the due date.

- **Anticipatory** breach – when one party informs the other party prior to the due date that the contract will not be completed. Compensation can be sought as soon as the innocent party is aware of the breach. Anticipatory breach is often referred to as **renunciation.**

Anticipatory breach may be express or implied:

- **Express** anticipatory breach occurs where one of the parties declares, before the due date for performance, that they have no intention of carrying out their contractual obligations.

- **Implied** anticipatory breach occurs where one of the parties does something which makes subsequent performance of their contractual undertaking impossible.

This section examines the legal remedies that may be available to any injured party as a result of a breach of contract.

3.2   Damages

The innocent party can claim damages from the guilty party. He may recover **damages** for any loss suffered as a result of the breach by bringing an **action for damages** for breach of contract. The objective of damages is to put the innocent person into the same financial position he would have been in if the contract had been completed correctly. The amount of damages awarded should compensate the innocent party but should not punish the guilty party.

If the breach consists of the other party's failure to pay a debt (i.e. the contractually agreed price or other remuneration due under the contract), the appropriate course for the injured party is to bring an action for the **agreed sum** to recover that amount, this is an **action for price.**

3.3   Equitable remedies

If damages are not sufficient then equitable remedies, such as *specific performance*, *injunctions or rescission*, may be awarded.

Specific performance – This is a court order to force the guilty party to positively complete his contractual obligations.

Injunction – This is a court order to force the guilty party to perform a negative obligation i.e. to cease doing something or to remove something that is in breach of contract.

Rescission – Restores the parties to their exact pre-contractual position.

3.4   Retention of title

The seller can add to the contract that the **'goods remain the property of the seller until payment has been received'**. This means that if there is non-payment that the seller retains the ownership of the goods. This is particularly useful if the receivable becomes insolvent as the seller maintains priority over the goods when monies are being paid.

🖉 Activity 7

The normal remedy for breach of contract due to non payment of the debt is:

A   Action for remedy

B   Action for the goods

C   Action for specific performance

D   Action for price

🖉 Activity 8

Retention of title is:

A   The right of the seller to retain ownership of the goods until payment is made

B   The right of the purchaser to retain ownership of the goods received

C   The right of the purchaser to expect that title is retained by the seller even when payment has been received

D   The right of the seller to retain ownership of the goods until a cheque has been posted

---

3.5   Late Payment of Commercial Debts (Interest) Act 1998

The late payment act allows businesses to **charge other business customers interest on overdue amounts** and allows businesses to cover late payments of bank borrowings. Interest can be charged:

- 30 days after the goods are supplied or the service is completed.

- 30 days after receipt of invoice (or the customer is told the amount due is payable).

- The agreed date for payment.

The interest rate is 8% above the Bank of England base rate for the period the debt is late. The interest is based on the VAT inclusive amount and calculated as a simple interest rate.

Example

A debt of £3,000 exclusive of VAT has been outstanding for 60 days. The Bank of England base rate is 0.5%. The late payment charge is:

3,000 × 1.2 × 0.085 × 60/365 = £50.30

3.6 Irrecoverable debt relief

If a business sells VAT taxable goods or services to a customer, the VAT element is paid to HMRC. If the customer does not pay for the goods or services irrecoverable debt relief can be claimed. For a business to be able to claim back the VAT that has been paid, the debt must:

- be more than six months old and less than four years and six months old

- be written off

- not have been sold or handed to a factoring company

- not be more than the normal selling price for the items.

4 Data Protection Act

4.1 Introduction

Due to the growth in the use of computer technology the Data Protection Act 1998 was introduced to make **certain restrictions** on the use of data about **individuals** and the **use of personal data**. It is likely that your organisation will hold computer data about credit customers and therefore you need to be aware of the broad outlines of the Act. However it is important to realise that the Act relates to data **held about individuals not about organisations** so will only be relevant to non-corporate customers or to data about individuals who belong to a customer organisation.

4.2 Definitions

Personal data is information held about an individual, not only factual information but also expressions of opinion about that individual.

Data users are individuals or organisations who use personal data.

A **computer bureau** is an individual or organisation which processes personal data for data users, or allows data users to process personal data on its equipment.

4.3   The key principles of the Act

- Data may only be used for the **specific purposes** for which it was collected.

- Data **must not be disclosed** to other parties without the consent of the individual whom it is about, unless there is legislation or other overriding legitimate reason to share the information (for example, the prevention or detection of crime). It is an offence for other parties to obtain this personal data without authorisation.

- **Individuals have a right of access to the information held about them,** subject to certain exceptions (for example, information held for the prevention or detection of crime).

- Personal information may be **kept for no longer than is necessary** and must be kept up to date.

- Personal information **may not be sent outside the European Economic Area** unless the individual whom it is about has consented or adequate protection is in place, for example, by the use of a prescribed form of contract to govern the transmission of the data.

- Subject to some exceptions for organisations that only do very simple processing, and for domestic use, all entities that process personal information must **register with the Information Commissioner's Office**.

- Entities holding personal information are required to have adequate **security measures in place**. Those include technical measures (such as firewalls) and organisational measures (such as staff training).

- Subjects have the right to have **factually incorrect information corrected** (note: this does not extend to matters of opinion).

- All data users and computer bureaux have to **register with the Data Protection Registrar** – the data user must then only hold data and use data for the purposes which are registered.

- Processing of personal data is forbidden except in the following circumstances:

    - with the consent of the individual

    - due to a legal obligation

    - due to a contractual obligation

    - due to a contractual arrangement

    - in the public interest

    - to protect the vital interests of the individual.

- If data is obtained from a third party the data subject must be given:
  - the identity of the controller of the data
  - the purposes for which the data is being processed
  - the data that will be disclosed and to whom.

- Data subjects have the right to a copy of the data held, the right to know why the data is being processed and the logic behind the processing. Data subjects may seek compensation through the courts for damage or distress caused by the loss, destruction, inaccuracy or unauthorised disclosure of personal data.

- Data subjects can apply to the courts or Registrar for inaccurate data to be corrected or removed from the data user's files.

Activity 9

The Data Protection Act applies to (pick as many as appropriate):

A   Data about individuals, companies and government departments

B   Data about individuals only

C   Data about companies only

D   Data about companies and individuals only

E   Only manual records

F   Only computer records

G   All records held by the company

H   Only records of opinions

5   Other legislation

5.1   Trade Descriptions Act

The Trade Descriptions Act states that manufacturers, retailers and the service industry must **correctly describe what they are selling**. The goods or service must be as described, of satisfactory quality and be fit for purpose. It is a **criminal offence to make a false or misleading statement** about the goods or services being provided i.e. **misrepresented** in any way.

5.2   Unfair Contract Terms Act

Contracts must be written in **language that is understandable** and any part of the contract that acts more favourably for the vendor than the consumer is unfair and not binding.

This is the most important statute affecting exclusion clauses and is largely restricted to business liability i.e. liability arising during business or from occupation of premises for business purposes. It is not possible to exclude liability for death or personal injury and all other losses are subject to a test of reasonableness.

5.3   Sale of Goods Act 1979

The sale of goods act **applies when the title of the goods has passed from the vendor to the buyer** and states that as a buyer you have 3 statutory rights:

1   The seller has the right to be selling the goods/providing the service.

2   That the goods match the description provided by the seller i.e. the goods are 'as described' and '**fit for purpose**'.

3   The goods are of '**satisfactory quality**'.

5.4   Consumer Credit Act 1974

The Consumer Credit Act 1974 requires:

- Businesses that offer goods or services on credit or lend money to individuals to be **licensed** by the **Office of Fair Trading.** Trading without a licensing arrangement is a criminal offence and can result in a fine and/or imprisonment.

- That the borrower can settle a regulated consumer credit agreement early by giving notice to the lender and paying the amount due less a rebate. The borrower is also entitled to information about the amount needed to settle.

- The seller lays down rules requiring information to be given to borrowers or hirers before entry into a consumer credit or hire agreement.

KAPLAN PUBLISHING

Activity 10

Calvin is sold some lime cordial by Hobbs but when Calvin opens the bottle it is actually lemonade. Calvin can claim for breach of contract due to:

A   Fiduciary misconduct

B   Misrepresentation

C   Misuse of Sales Act

D   Unfair Contract Terms Act

6   Summary

The sale of goods on credit to a customer is a contract and therefore you need to be aware of the legal background in terms of the general nature of contract law. You must also be aware of the basic provisions of the Data Protection Act and other legal terms and conditions in relation to a contract.

Answers to chapter activities

Activity 1

Answer D

Activity 2

Answer C

Activity 3

Answer C

Activity 4

Answer D

Activity 5

Answer C

Activity 6

Answer D

Activity 7

Answer D

Activity 8

Answer A

Activity 9

Answers B and G

Activity 10

Answer B

7 Test your knowledge

Workbook Activity 11

Steph has asked Callum for a price to paint her bedroom. Callum has said he can do it for £300 and Steph has agreed. Nearing the end of the job Callum asks Steph for £50 more as he has underestimated the work.

Does Steph have to pay Callum the extra £50?

Yes / No ?

Workbook Activity 12

Tina orders a Chinese takeaway over the telephone and says she will pay on delivery. Which of the following would constitute consideration?

A   Handing over the money to the delivery driver

B   Promising to pay for the takeaway

C   Accepting delivery of the takeaway

D   Calling the Chinese takeaway

Granting credit

2

Introduction

In this chapter we look at why a business grants credit and what information is required to decide whether to grant credit or extend credit terms and conditions.

<table>
<tr><td colspan="2">ASSESSMENT CRITERIA</td></tr>
<tr><td colspan="2">Identify sources of credit status and related information used to assess the risk of granting credit (2.1K)</td></tr>
<tr><td colspan="2">Explain methods of assessing credit control information (2.2K)</td></tr>
<tr><td colspan="2">Assess the current credit status of customers and potential customers (2.3S)</td></tr>
<tr><td colspan="2">Agree credit terms with new customers or changes to credit terms with existing customers (2.4S)</td></tr>
<tr><td colspan="2">Communicate tactfully the reasons for refusing or extending credit with customers (2.5S)</td></tr>
</table>

CONTENTS

1 Granting credit
2 External sources of information
3 Internal sources of information
4 Analysis of accounts
5 Liquidity ratios
6 Profitability ratios
7 Debt ratios
8 Cash flow ratios
9 Example and activities
10 Overtrading
11 Credit terms and conditions
12 Refusal of credit

1 Granting credit

1.1 Introduction

Payment for goods can either be made by cash or credit. Payment by **cash** (including cheque, credit/debit cards) means that the business received what it is owed for the goods or services at the time they are provided. Payment on **credit** where an invoice is raised means that the business provides the goods or service and payment is received later. This creates trade receivables for the business – customers who owe the business money.

1.2 The trade receivable balancing act

Trade receivables are people who owe business money, the almost inevitable consequence of trading. Trade receivables form part of the **working capital cycle** and as such management of trade receivables is very important in **maintaining the liquidity** of the company.

For many businesses their entire turnover is made on credit terms with very few business-to-business transactions being made for cash and likewise fewer business-to-customer transactions are cash.

Trade receivable management principles involve a series of balancing acts. The following diagram should be remembered.

Balancing costs and benefits of trade receivables

Benefit of granting trade credit	Costs of granting trade credit
	Finance costs
Marketing benefits	Irrecoverable debts costs (default)
	Administration costs

The main benefit to the company is that **customers like to be given trade credit**, rather than paying on delivery of goods. Thus, generous credit terms often have a beneficial impact on sales.

Giving a customer credit terms for payment is always a risk and all companies try to reduce this risk and potential irrecoverable debt problems.

1.3 Credit control

The following need to be in place to reduce the risks associated with granting credit:

- The **credit manager** protects the company's investment in trade receivables. This entails ensuring appropriate credit terms are negotiated with customers and are then adhered to. The manager usually reports to the finance director or financial controller; sometimes, however, he may be found within the sales/marketing area.

- A company policy – the credit manager needs to ascertain the basis of the **company's credit terms**. This may have been decided upon by the finance director or has to be developed by the credit controller in consultation with his superior and the sales department. This has the advantage of allowing a flexible method to develop which can cater for differing situations.

- Consideration needs to be given to the **nature of the market** and any **seasonal fluctuations**, the expected level of sales, the marketing strategy and the policies of competitors.

- It must be clear who **establishes the credit terms**: the sales manager or the credit manager, or both in consultation – in which case, their joint policy must be clearly documented to avoid any misunderstandings. Also, the credit manager needs to establish whether he has the authority to accept or reject new customers or new orders.

- The correct **evaluation of credit risk** is the most difficult and the most vital part of the credit manager's role. It is not only new accounts that need to be considered, the credit manager needs constantly to **review his established customer base** to ensure that they continue to be a safe risk and have not slipped with their payments.

There are various ways of obtaining information about customers both from one's own experience and from internal and external sources and references. All available information needs to be collected and assimilated so that appropriate credit terms can be given to the customer. Once agreed, these terms will then form the basis of the contract of sale between the two parties and trading can proceed smoothly.

2 External sources of information

2.1 Trade credit references

Traditionally, creditworthiness has been checked by asking the customer to supply trade references from **two other suppliers**. As it can be assumed that customers will not quote suppliers likely to give a bad report, it is **unwise to rely on this procedure alone**. Beware of companies that pay their two referee suppliers promptly, but pay all other suppliers late. Used in conjunction with other information, this procedure however may be helpful.

Trade reference requests should be made **formally** and should ask for credit terms. Often a standard form can be used requesting:

- the exact name of the potential customer
- the usual credit terms offered
- the expected level of business
- names and addresses of two trade referees.

From this information, the credit manager can contact the trade referees and ensure the potential customer can pay on time and adhere to agreed credit terms.

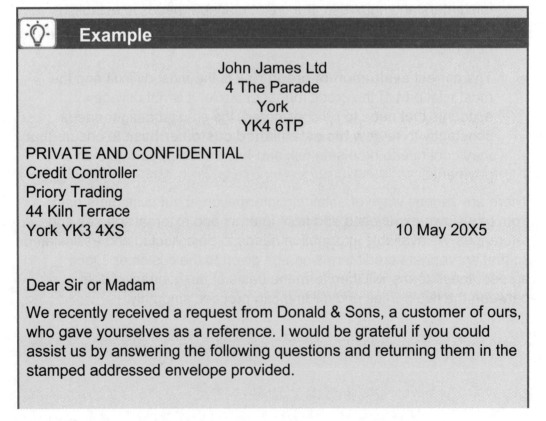

> **Example**
>
> John James Ltd
> 4 The Parade
> York
> YK4 6TP
>
> PRIVATE AND CONFIDENTIAL
> Credit Controller
> Priory Trading
> 44 Kiln Terrace
> York YK3 4XS   10 May 20X5
>
>
> Dear Sir or Madam
>
> We recently received a request from Donald & Sons, a customer of ours, who gave yourselves as a reference. I would be grateful if you could assist us by answering the following questions and returning them in the stamped addressed envelope provided.

1   How long have Donald & Sons been trading with you?

     2 years   months

2   When Donald & Sons opened an account with you, did the
     company supply you with suitable trade and credit references?

     YES / (NO)

3   What are your normal credit terms for Donald & Sons?

     Amount: £10,000

     Terms: Cash   Weekly   (Monthly)   Other

4   Does Donald & Sons make payments in accordance with your
     terms?

     (YES)/ NO / SLOW PAYER

5   Have you ever had to suspend credit facilities to Donald & Sons?

     YES / (NO)

     If Yes, when?

6   Please supply any other information which you consider relevant.

Thank you for your help.

Yours faithfully

B Down

B Down
Brian Down Credit Controller Solution

2.2   Bank references

It is usual to take up bank references at the same time as trade
references. Requests to the bank need to be **precise**, detailing the
amount of credit you envisage giving the customer and the **credit
period**. Bank replies are usually structured in one of three ways:

(1)   an **unqualified**, **positive** assurance

(2)   a **general indication** that the firm is operating normally

(3)   a **guarded statement**, indicating that 'capital is fully employed' or
      'we are unable to speak for your figures'.

It is always useful to speak to the bank on the telephone as more
information may be conveyed via word of mouth. However, a reference of
the latter type should put the credit manager on guard.

⚡ **Example**

Northern Bank plc

Doncaster Branch
501 High Street
Doncaster DN3 4XL

Credit Controller
John James Ltd
4 The Parade
York YK4 6TP

19 May 20X5

Dear Sir or Madam

Reference: Donald & Sons

I refer to your letter dated 10 May 20X5 enquiring about the creditworthiness of the above. In our view, Donald & Sons is reasonably constituted and should prove good for your figures.

Yours faithfully

G Donarski

Gerald Donarski
Manager

📝 **Activity 1**

When taking up bank references they usually provide one of 3 types of references. Which of the following is not a standard bank reference?

A   Unqualified, positive

B   Qualified, positive

C   Guarded

D   General indication

2.3 Credit reference agency reports

Credit agencies are not covered by the Data Protection Act but by the Consumer Credit Act 1974 which actually gives stronger protection in terms of the handling of information.

One of the most widely used registers is that of Dun & Bradstreet. It summarises data for over 210 million businesses in over 200 countries, including the **name, address, date of formation, nominal and issued share capital, existing mortgages and charges, proprietors and associates, credit rating** and Dun & Bradstreet rating.

The vital piece of information for the credit manager is the **credit rating** which indicates the **average amount of credit given to the firm**. This helps the credit manager to assess the relative size of the proposed credit limit to the potential customer. If this is much greater than the average listed, it would be advisable to undertake further investigations.

The usefulness of a report from an agency depends on the skill and competence of the agency. A specialised agency for the particular industry concerned can normally offer more detached information, but the credit manager needs to research the agency carefully. If he is satisfied that they have experienced, trained staff, the report is based on up-to-date information and they produce reports for other reputable firms, then confidence may be placed in their findings.

The questions of cost and speed of reporting should not be considered as agencies who offer low-cost reports are immediately suspect. Worthwhile reports cannot be produced cheaply and, although speed is important, it is very difficult to specify minimum reporting periods for gathering information from so many different sources.

The credit manager should look for the following **contents** in the report on the potential customer:

- name and address; associated companies with names and addresses
- name of proprietors, partners and/or directors
- amount of authorised and issued share capital
- description of the customer's activities
- latest statement of financial position and statement of profit or loss
- a list of secured charges and mortgages
- name and address of its financial advisers, bankers
- payment pattern/experience from other suppliers
- a recommended credit limit based on the findings in the report.

The **problems** with agency reports are as follows:

- **New companies have no track record**. It is therefore very difficult to form a judgement.

- It takes time for current information to be analysed and fed into computer/appraisal systems. It is possible for very relevant information (such as the collapse of a major customer) not to be in a report.

- Suppliers' references may be too old to be of value.

2.4 Statutory accounts

Historical financial information can provide information on the financial position of a business – the levels of profitability and liquidity it has maintained in the previous years.

It may also be possible to access the management accounts of a business if they are provided by the customer.

2.5 Credit circle reports

A credit circle is a **group of people** with a common interest for example a trade association. These people meet on a regular basis to **share information on credit related matters**, such as late payers or bad trade receivables.

This information is both useful for current credit customers – are the customers struggling to pay other debts? – and potential credit customers – what is their/has their credit management been like?

2.6 Official publications

The press provide an **up-to-date commentary** on the situation within local and national companies. If the proposed customer is a big national company, reading The Financial Times enables the credit manager to keep up-to-date with half-yearly reports, comments on the customer as well as keeping abreast of industry trends and problems. Smaller more local companies are commented upon in regional and local papers.

Often produced weekly or monthly, **trade journals** are another valuable source of information and **commentary on trends and results**.

3 Internal sources of information

3.1 Introduction

A company's sales ledger, where each sale is recorded and all payments from customers are noted, will be one of the main internal sources of information.

The sales ledger will provide the basis for investigation of:

- Trading history of existing credit customers.

- Aged receivables analysis.

- Irrecoverable debts.

Effective monitoring of trade receivable balances can only occur if the accounts information is correct.

3.2 Trading history

An overview or investigation into a **company's trading history** can be a very useful tool when deciding to extend credit terms or limits. It can show how long a company has been in operation and how well trading has been going.

3.3 Aged analysis of trade receivables

Aged trade receivable analysis is used to assess the status of **current credit** customers.

Definition

The aged analysis of trade receivables analyses the **balance due** from each trade receivable according to the amount of time that each individual invoice has been outstanding.

The credit manager should closely monitor the collection of debts. The aged trade receivable analysis allows speedy perusal of old/slow paying trade receivables which facilitates prompt action.

The report is usually produced at the **end of each month** alongside the monthly statements. It splits the total outstanding balance into differing age categories, for example:

(a) amounts less than one month old

(b)   amounts between one and two months old

(c)   amounts between two and three months old

(d)   amounts over three months old.

It is also useful to print the customer's credit limit alongside this information.

The credit manager should be aware of customers who:

(a)   are building up a significant outstanding account i.e. are slow payers

(b)   have exceeded their credit limit

(c)   have not paid for a long period of time

(d)   have a strange pattern in their payments i.e. recent debts are cleared but there is an older outstanding amount.

3.4   Irrecoverable debts

An **irrecoverable debt** is a debt which the credit manager is fairly certain will never be received from the customer.

A **specific allowance for doubtful debts** is a provision against a particular debt owed as there is concern that it may not be paid in full.

A **general allowance** is a further provision against a percentage of remaining debts which reflects the fact that some debts may not be paid in full.

If a credit customer has had a provision applied to its account for an irrecoverable debt or a doubtful debt it would not be sensible to look at extending credit terms.

3.5   Sales representatives' knowledge

A company's sales representatives will have **first hand information** on existing customers and may have met or known of potential customers, all of which is useful to the credit manager.

It is beneficial to the credit manager to train the sales staff to observe and listen for information on customers' ability to pay by finding out:

- the level of activity at the factory
- the impression/competence of the customer's staff and premises
- the names of other suppliers
- future plans of the customer/client
- any other information possible.

This provides more **background information to analyse** alongside other facts, though the credit manager would need to be mindful of the sales representatives' optimism!

3.6 Analysis of accounts

One of the most useful sources of external information are the **annual accounts** of the customer (if it is a company). From these, various statistics can be calculated **internally** to help to analyse the company's situation. However, it must be remembered that the financial accounts only give **historic data** and it is often the case that the most recent accounts available from companies are at least 12 months out of date.

Whatever accounts are produced for examination, it is necessary to **respect the confidential nature** of the documents and the credit manager must exercise due care in this regard.

The calculations for this are looked at in more detail later in this chapter.

3.7 80/20 rule

Analysis of trade receivables can be simplified using Pareto's Principle or the 80/20 rule. Vilfredo Pareto noted that 20% of the people in Italy owned 80% of the country's wealth.

If this principle is applied to the trade receivables of a company it could help the credit manager focus the credit control team. The credit manager could assume that 80% of the debts owed in value were due to only 20% of the customer accounts thereby focusing attention and analysis on these 20% of customers.

3.8 Materiality

Another way to assess trade receivables is on the materiality of the debt or the value of debt in comparison to total value of trade receivables. If one debt is the majority of the trade receivables then attentions needs to be focused on receiving that money.

The credit manager also needs to consider the cost of collecting the debt in comparison to the value of the debt. A small outstanding amount may cost more to collect than it is actually worth to the business.

Activity 2

In gathering credit information on a potential client you would use both internal sources of credit information and external sources of credit information. Which of the following is an example of internal information?

A   Trade references

B   Sales representatives' knowledge

C   Credit agency

D   Bank references

📝 Activity 3

Which of the following is not a method of analysing credit control information?

A   Aged trade payable analysis

B   Pareto's Principle

C   Key performance indicators

D   Trading history

3.9 How to use the information

There are variously sources of information that can be used to analyse trade receivables; most of these have been discussed earlier in the chapter.

When analysing current credit customers you may need to decide on which customers to focus the debt collection efforts on.

When deciding whether or not to grant credit to a customer you will need to be able to analyse any information gathered.

Some of the techniques mentioned are more useful for current credit customers, some for potential credit customers and some are more useful for analysing both:

Current credit customers	Potential credit customers	Current and potential credit customers
Aged trade receivable analysis	Trade references	Credit circle reports
80/20 rule	Bank references	Performance indicators
Materiality		Trading history
Sales ledger information		Credit rating agencies
		Press reports
		Trade journals
		Status reports
		Sale representatives knowledge

Activity 4

Which of the following information should be used to assess the credit status of a new customer?

(i)   Aged trade receivable analysis

(ii)   Draft contract for trade

(iii)   Trade references

(iv)   Bank references

(v)   Financial accounts

(vi)   Copies of outstanding invoices

A   All of the above

B   (iii) only

C   (iii), (iv) and (v) only

D   (ii) and (v) only

Activity 5

Which of the following would be used to assess the credit status of a current customer?

(i)   Aged trade receivable analysis

(ii)   Draft contract for trade

(iii)   Trade references

(iv)   Bank references

(v)   Financial accounts

(vi)   Copies of outstanding invoices

A   (i) only

B   (i), (v) and (vi) only

C   (v) and (vi) only

D   All of the above

4 Analysis of accounts

4.1 Key performance indicators

Key performance indicators can be calculated to analyse financial accounts provided by a business. There are four aspects of a company's performance that the credit manager should consider:

- **Liquidity** – the ability of the company to pay its debts from its current assets, i.e. there are sufficient liquid resources.

- **Profitability** – this is obviously important as, in the long run, an unprofitable company will not survive.

- **Debt** – this is concerned with risk. How much capital (equity) is there compared to debt (loans).

- **Cash flow** – different calculations to assess liquidity.

This information can be used to decide on whether to **offer credit terms** to a new company or whether to **extend credit terms** to a current credit customer. With current credit customers it is also a useful tool to be able to **assess how the business is progressing** – have ratios improved or worsened. This could lead to a **change in credit policy** being implemented.

Before examining the various accounting ratios in detail, it is important to remember that:

(a) an opinion cannot be formed from one year's statistics alone – it is more useful to develop trends for several years/months before concluding

(b) it is helpful to be able to compare the company's statistics with other companies in the same industrial sector – hopefully the company concerned will be better than average

(c) the accounts may be distorted due to inter-company transactions, group funding etc. and so an opinion can only be formed by looking at the accounts for the whole group

(d) statistics are only statistics! It is very easy in recessionary or inflationary times for the position of a company to change very quickly from profitable to loss making, so the credit manager must not become blinded by numbers alone.

The next few sections work through each of the assessable areas of a business and provides the calculations that can be used.

5 Liquidity ratios

5.1 Current ratio

This is a common method of analysing working capital and is generally accepted as the measure of **short-term liquidity**. It indicates the extent to which the current liabilities of a business are covered by the current assets.

$$\text{Current ratio} = \frac{\text{Current assets}}{\text{Current liabilities}}$$

The aim is to ensure that current liabilities can be met as they fall due. This ratio can be shown as X:1 but should be shown as X in the CBT. Sometimes, textbooks suggest that if the current ratio is below a certain level (which is usually given as between 1.5 and 2), the business should become seriously concerned.

This should not be taken to be a strict rule, because:

(a) current liabilities include the bank overdraft which, in practice, is not repayable within one year (technically, of course, repayable on demand)

(b) different types of industry will have different typical current ratios. For example a supermarket will have high payable levels and high inventories but very few trade receivables; whereas a manufacturing business will not only have high payable and inventory levels but also significant levels of trade receivables.

Even considering the points above a current ratio of below 1:1 would be of concern to any business as it indicates that there are insufficient assets to cover the current liabilities as they fall due.

5.2 Quick ratio

The quick ratio is also known as the **acid test ratio**. It is calculated in the same way as for the current ratio but inventories are excluded from current assets.

$$\text{Quick ratio} = \frac{\text{Current assets} - \text{Inventory}}{\text{Current liabilities}}$$

This ratio can be shown as X:1 but should be shown as X in the CBT.

This ratio is a much better test of the **immediate liquidity** of a business because inventory is assumed to be the least liquid of the current assets due to the length of time necessary to convert it into cash (via sales and trade receivables).

Although increasing liquid resources more usually indicate favourable trading, it could be that funds are not being used to their best advantage (e.g. a large unused cash balance).

As with the current ratio, a quick ratio of less than 1:1 would be of concern to a business.

5.3 Accounts receivable collection period

Also known as the trade receivables' ratio.

$$\text{Average collection period (in days)} = \frac{\text{Trade receivables}}{\text{Sales revenue}} \times 365$$

When using the above formula we have to assume that all sales have been made on credit. If a **credit sales** figure is provided then this is a more accurate figure to use in the calculation of the accounts receivable collection period.

This indicates the length of time it takes the company **to receive the cash from its credit customers**. This is not directly relevant to the decision whether or not to grant credit but it can give useful information about how the company's credit control department operates.

5.4 Accounts payable payment period

Also known as the trade payables' ratio.

$$\text{Average payment period (in days)} = \frac{\text{Trade payables}}{\text{Cost of sales}} \times 365$$

When using the above formula we have to assume that the cost of sales is representative of the credit purchases. If a **credit purchases** figure is provided then this is a more accurate figure to use in the calculation of the accounts payable payment period.

This ratio is **directly relevant** to the decision whether or not to grant credit as it indicates the length of time a company takes to **pay its current credit suppliers.**

It is desirable for the trade receivables' collection period to be shorter than the trade payables' payment period. This way the company collects what is due before it has to pay out to its own trade payables.

5.5 Inventory holding period in days

This ratio indicates whether a business's inventories are justified in relation to its sales. It estimates how long inventory is held in the business before it is sold.

$$\text{Inventory holding period (in days)} = \frac{\text{Inventory}}{\text{Cost of sales}} \times 365$$

If the inventory holding period increases this may indicate excess inventories or sluggish sales.

 6 **Profitability ratios**

6.1 Gross profit margin

This ratio isolates the pure 'nuts and bolts' of a business, i.e. the sales revenue and what it costs to make those sales.

$$\text{Gross Margin (\%)} = \frac{\text{Gross profit}}{\text{Sales revenue}} \times 100$$

A low margin indicates low sales revenue and/ or high costs.

6.2 Profit for the period margin (operating profit margin)

This ratio includes the other costs incurred in running a business.

$$\text{Operating profit (\%)} = \frac{\text{Operating profit}}{\text{Sales revenue}} \times 100$$

A low margin indicates low selling prices or high costs or both.

6.3 Return on capital employed

Capital employed is normally measured as **equity plus non-current liabilities** (or, alternatively, **non-current assets plus current assets minus current liabilities**); it represents the long-term investment in the business.

Return on capital employed is frequently regarded as the **best measure** of profitability, indicating how successful a business is in utilising its assets.

This ratio is only meaningful when the true values of assets are known and used in the formula.

$$\text{Return on capital employed} = \frac{\text{Operating profit}}{\text{Capital employed}} \times 100$$

A low return on capital employed is caused by either a low profit margin or a low asset turnover or both.

The aim is to see how effectively the business is using the money invested in it.

Care should be taken with the interpretation of this ratio for the following reasons:

- It is based upon the statement of financial position values of the net assets rather than the true market value i.e. depreciation has been charged against the cost of the assets.

- A high ROCE may be solely due to accounting for depreciation reducing the capital employed figure rather than a high profit figure.

- As the statement of financial position values are based upon historical cost then the age structure of the assets of the business can also affect the return on capital employed.

- Often new investment does not bring immediate profits. This may be for a number of reasons. It may take time for the company's employees to learn how to use the new equipment. Alternatively it may take the company time to obtain enough orders to use the new facilities to the full. (This may result in a temporary reduction in the ROCE).

6.4 Interest cover

This provides the ratio of Profit before interest to the interest charged on loans or the Finance cost.

$$\text{Interest cover} = \frac{\text{Profit before interest}}{\text{Finance cost}}$$

Interest cover is expressed as a number, e.g. 4 times. It gives an indication of how easily the company can maintain payments of its loan and debenture interest and therefore gives additional information about the riskiness of the company. A rough guide would be to assume that if the interest cover is 2 times then we can assume that profit could halve and interest payments can still be made. Anything lower than 2 would indicate a risky situation.

The purpose of the assessment of the customer's financial statements is to determine the likelihood that they will pay their trade debts on time. If a company has long-term loan capital in its capital structure, then the interest on this must be paid thereby reducing the profits available to make other payments such as those to trade payables. Therefore the interest cover is additional evidence of the risk associated with the company.

7 Debt ratios

7.1 Gearing ratio

Here we are trying to assess the composition of a company's capital structure – is the business being funded by equity (repayable to shareholders) or by debt (repayable to banks). If there is a lot of debt compared to the equity it is thought that a business is riskier as debt must be paid back to the banks when requested whereas equity does not have to be paid back to the shareholders on demand. The greater the extent to which a company is financed by debt, the greater is the risk involved in allowing it credit terms.

$$\text{Gearing ratio} = \frac{\text{Total debt}}{\text{Total debt} + \text{equity}} \times 100$$

or

$$\text{Gearing ratio} = \frac{\text{Total debt}}{\text{Total equity}} \times 100$$

Examination points:

- both calculations are allowed in the exam

- total debt could include short term debt (overdrafts) and long term debt (loans). Legally an overdraft is repayable on demand so it is classified as a current liability (short term debt). In reality a business will have an overdraft for greater than one year meaning it is considered long term debt. Trade payables do not need to be included.

7.2 Short term debt ratio

This ratio assesses the amount of short-term debt in the company. Short-term debt has to be paid back within the year. So this can be another element of the risk for a company.

$$\text{Short term debt ratio} = \frac{\text{Short term debt}}{\text{Total debt}} \times 100$$

8 Cash flow ratios

8.1 Cash flow ratios

The most important asset for a company to have to be able to meet its debt requirement is cash. The following calculations are similar to some of the ones above but the profit figure is adjusted for values that are calculated due to accounting concepts.

> **Definition**
>
> **EBITDA** – Earnings before interest, tax, depreciation and amortisation is **profit but with accounting concepts such as accruals, depreciation removed** to give an indication of cash flow.

8.2 EBITDA interest cover

Using a statement of profit or loss:

$$\text{Interest cover} = \frac{\text{EBITDA}}{\text{Finance cost}}$$

Or using a cash flow statement:

$$\text{Interest cover} = \frac{\text{EBITDA}}{\text{Interest paid}}$$

8.3 EBITDA to total debt

$$= \frac{\text{EBITDA}}{\text{Total debt}} \times 100$$

EBITDA formulae give an indication of how cash relates to the expenditure requirements of a business.

9 Example and activities

9.1 Example

> ### Example
>
> The following illustration demonstrates some of the ratios with which you need to be familiar when assessing credit risk.
>
> **Summarised statement of financial position at 31 December 20X1**
>
> | | £000 | £000 |
> |---|---|---|
> | **Non-current assets**, at cost, less depreciation | | 2,600 |
> | **Current assets** | | |
> | Inventory | 600 | |
> | Trade receivables | 900 | |
> | Cash and other equivalents | 100 | |
> | | ——— | |
> | | | 1,600 |
> | | | ——— |
> | **Total Assets** | | **4,200** |
> | | | |
> | **Equity** | | |
> | Ordinary share capital (£1 shares) | | 1,000 |
> | Preference share capital | | 200 |
> | Retained earnings | | 800 |
> | | | ——— |
> | | | 2,000 |
> | **Non-current liabilities** | | |
> | Loan | | 1,400 |
> | **Current liabilities** | | |
> | Trade payables | 800 | |
> | | ——— | |
> | | | 800 |
> | | | ——— |
> | **Total equity and liabilities** | | **4,200** |

Summarised statement of profit or loss for the year ended 31 December 20X1

	20X1
	£000
Revenue	6,000
Cost of sales	(4,000)
Gross profit	2,000
Operating expenses	(1,660)
Operating profit	340
Finance cost	(74)
Profit before tax	266
Taxation	(106)
	160
Preference dividend	(10)
Profit for the year	150

Note that cost of sales and operating expenses include £600,000 of depreciation charges.

Solution

Liquidity ratios

Current ratio

$$\text{Current ratio} = \frac{\text{Current assets}}{\text{Current liabilities}} = \frac{£1,600}{£800} = 2$$

Quick ratio

$$\text{Quick ratio} = \frac{\text{Current assets} - \text{Inventory}}{\text{Current liabilities}} = \frac{£1,600 - £600}{£800} = 1.25$$

Accounts receivable collection period

$$\text{Average collection period} = \frac{\text{Trade receivables}}{\text{Sales revenue}} \times 365$$

$$= \frac{£900}{£6,000} \times 365 = 55 \text{ days}$$

Accounts payable collection period

$$\text{Average payment period} = \frac{\text{Trade payables}}{\text{Cost of sales}} \times 365$$

$$= \frac{£800}{£4,000} \times 365 = 73 \text{ days}$$

Inventory holding period in days

$$\text{Inventory turnover} = \frac{\text{Inventory}}{\text{Cost of sales}} \times 365$$

$$= \frac{£600}{£4,6000} \times 365 = 55 \text{ days}$$

Profitability ratios

Gross profit margin

$$\text{Margin} = \frac{\text{Gross profit}}{\text{Sales revenue}} \times 100 = \frac{£2,000}{£6,000} \times 100 = 33.33\%$$

Profit for the period margin

$$\text{Margin} = \frac{\text{Operating profit}}{\text{Sales revenue}} \times 100$$

$$= \frac{£340}{£6,000} \times 100 = 5.67\%$$

Interest cover

$$\text{Finance charge cover} = \frac{\text{Profit before interest}}{\text{Interest payable}}$$

$$= \frac{£340}{£74} = 4.6 \text{ times}$$

Return on capital employed

$$\text{Return on capital employed} = \frac{\text{Operating profit}}{\text{Capital employed}} \times 100$$

$$= \frac{£340}{£2,000 + £1,400} \times 100 = 10\%$$

Gearing ratio

$$\text{Gearing ratio} = \frac{\text{Total debt}}{\text{Total debt + equity}} \times 100$$

$$= \frac{£1,400}{£2,000 + £1,400} \times 100 = 41.18\%$$

9.2 Activities

Activity 6

Summarised statement of financial position at 31 December 20X1

	£000	£000
Non-current assets, at cost, less depreciation		2,500
Current assets		
Inventory	900	
Trade receivables	800	
Cash and other equivalents	300	
		2,000
Total Assets		**4,500**
Equity		
Ordinary shares (£1 shares)		1,000
Preference shares		250
General reserve		600
Retained earnings		150
		2,000
Non-current liabilities		
10% debentures (loan)		1,500
Current liabilities		
Trade payables	700	
Other payables	300	
		1,000
Total equity and liabilities		**4,500**

Statement of profit or loss for year ended 31 December 20X1

	£000	£000
Revenue		6,000
Cost of sales		
Inventory at 1 January	500	
Purchases	4,000	
	4,500	
Less: inventory at 31 December 20X1	(900)	
		(3,600)
Gross profit		2,400
Administrative expenses and distribution costs		(1,830)
Operating profit		570
Finance cost		(150)
Profit before tax		420
Taxation		(210)
		210
Preference dividend		(10)
Profit for the year		200

Required

Calculate:

- Return on capital employed
- Operating profit margin
- Current ratio
- Quick ratio
- Receivable days
- Payable days
- Inventory days
- Gearing ratio (Total debt/Total debt + Equity)
- Interest cover.

As mentioned earlier in the chapter, one set of performance indicator calculations is not really enough to draw conclusions from. Many companies will request a couple of years of accounts to perform calculations on to see how the business under investigation has changed.

Another method is to have a credit rating (scoring) system to be able to grade a company's credit risk.

Activity 7

The accounts of Falcon Limited for the years ended 30 June 20X3 and 30 June 20X2 are as follows.

Statement of financial position

	20X3 £	20X3 £	20X2 £	20X2 £
Non-current assets				
Property		125,000		75,000
Plant		130,000		70,000
		255,000		145,000
Current assets				
Inventory	120,000		100,000	
Trade receivables	80,000		60,000	
		200,000		160,000
Total assets		455,000		305,000
Equity				
£1 ordinary shares		100,000		50,000
Share premium account		90,000		35,000
Retained earnings		135,000		120,000
		325,000		205,000
Non-current liabilities				
7% Loan		50,000		50,000
Current liabilities				
Trade payables	45,000		30,000	
Overdraft	15,000		5,000	
Taxation	20,000		15,000	
		80,000		50,000
Total equity and liabilities		455,000		305,000

Statement of profit or loss

	20X3 £	20X2 £
Revenue	525,000	425,000
Operating profit	53,500	41,000
Finance cost	(3,500)	(3,500)
Profit before tax	50,000	37,500
Tax	(20,000)	(15,000)
	30,000	22,500
Dividends	(15,000)	(10,000)
Profit for the year	15,000	12,500

Credit rating (scoring) system	Score
Operating profit margin	
losses	–5
less than 5%	0
5% and above but less than 10%	5
10% and above but less than 20%	10
more than 20%	20
Interest cover	
no cover	–30
less than 1	–20
more than 1 but less than 2	–10
more than 2 but less than 4	0
more than 4	10
Current ratio	
less than 1	–20
between 1 and 1.25	–10
between 1.25 and 1.5	0
above 1.5	10

Gearing (total debt/(total debt plus equity))	
less than 25%	20
25% and above but less than 50%	10
more than 50% less than 65%	0
between 65% and 75%	−20
between 75% and 80%	−40
above 80%	−100
Risk	**aggregate score**
very low risk	Between 60 and 21
low risk	Between 20 and 1
medium risk	Between 0 and −24
high risk	Between −25 and −50
very high risk	Above −50

Required

Calculate the performance indicators listed below and using the credit rating system calculate the risk of having Falcon Limited as a payable

	Indicator	Rating	Indicator	Rating
Year	20X3		20X2	
Operating profit margin				
Interest cover				
Current ratio				
Gearing				
Total				

Activity 8

Jacket and Tie have been trading with your company for several years and has, until recently, always paid to terms. Recently there have been a couple of late payments and Jacket and Tie have contacted you asking to increase their credit limit from £50,000 to £75,000.

Jacket and Tie have supplied the accounts below:

Statement of profit or loss

	20X1 £	20X2 £
Sales revenue	350,000	230,000
Cost of sales	(227,500)	(149,500)
Gross profit	122,500	80,500
Distribution costs	(25,000)	(20,000)
Administration costs	(50,000)	(45,000)
Operating profit	47,500	15,500
Finance cost	(5,000)	(5,000)
Profit before tax	42,500	10,500
Tax	(6,000)	(5,000)
Profit for the year	36,500	5,500

Statement of financial position

	20X1 £	20X2 £
Non-current assets	50,000	100,000
Current assets		
Inventory	25,690	18,164
Trade receivables	62,789	41,918
Cash	35,878	500
	124,357	60,582
Total assets	174,357	160,582
Equity		
Share capital	70,000	70,000
Retained earnings	43,418	22,418
	113,418	92,418
Non-current assets		
Loans	15,000	50,000
Current liabilities		
Short term loan	21,959	
Trade payable	23,980	18,164
	45,939	18,164
Total equity and liabilities	174,357	160,582

Jacket and Tie have also provided you with some further information:

We have recently succeeded in securing the business of several new large clients so we have had to purchase new assets with a long term loan to ensure that we can meet demand

We expect sales to increase next year but for our costs to stay constant as we are able to reduce variable costs through the use of our new machines.

Using the template provided:

1   Calculate the key indicators for the current and previous years for Jacket and Tie

Jacket and Tie	Indicator 20X1	Indicator 20X2
Operating profit margin		
Interest cover		
Current ratio		
Gearing		
Trade receivable days		
Trade payable days		

2   Analyse the ratios and the financial statements and discuss whether extension of the credit limit is feasible. You may want to consider adding terms to the contract.

Activity 9

You work as a credit controller and Sort Me Out Limited is asking for credit terms. They would like a credit limit of £750,000. Sort Me Out Limited have provided their financial accounts for the last two year.

Statement of profit or loss	20X2	20X1
	£000	£000
Revenue	5,500	6,500
Cost of sales	3,500	3,800
Gross profit	2,000	2,700
Distribution costs	1,250	2,150
Administration costs	1,000	1,000
Operating profit	–250	–450
Interest payable	50	50
Profit before taxation	–300	–500
Tax	0	0
Profit for the year	–300	–500

Statement of financial position	20X2	20X1
	£000	£000
Non-current assets		
Tangible assets	3,200	3,500
Current assets		
Inventories	1,000	800
Trade Receivables	1,100	950
Cash	100	500
	2,200	2,250
Total assets	5,400	5,750
Equity		
Share capital	200	200
Retained earnings	1,900	3,050
	2,100	3,250
Non-current liabilities		
Long term loans	1,000	500
Current liabilities		
Trade payables	2,300	2,000
Total liabilities	3,300	2,500
Total equity and liabilities	5,400	5,750

Credit rating (scoring) system	Score
Operating profit margin	
losses	−5
less than 5%	0
5% and above but less than 10%	5
10% and above but less than 20%	10
20% and above	20
Interest cover	
no cover	−30
less than 1	−20
1 and above but less than 2	−10
2 and above but less than 4	0
4 and above	10
Current ratio	
less than 1	−20
1 and above and less than 1.25	−10
1.25 and above and less than 1.5	0
1.5 and above	10
Gearing (total debt/(total debt plus equity))	
less than 25%	20
25% and above but less than 50%	10
50% and above and less than 65%	0
65% and above and less than 75%	−20
75% and above and less than 80%	−40
80% and above	−100

Risk	aggregate score
very low risk	Between 60 and 21
low risk	Between 20 and 1
medium risk	Between 0 and –24
high risk	Between –25 and –50
very high risk	Above –50

Calculate the performance indicators below for Sort Me Out Limited

Sort Me Out Limited	Indicator	Rating	Indicator	Rating
Year	20X2		20X1	
Operating profit margin				
Interest cover				
Current ratio				
Gearing				
Total				

Will we offer credit terms to Sort Me Out Limited?

Activity 10

You work as a credit controller and Help Me Out Limited is asking for credit terms. They would like a credit limit of £750,000. Help Me Out Limited has provided their financial accounts for the two previous years.

Statement of financial position

	20X1 £000	20X0 £000
Non-current assets		
Property, plant and equipment	7,000	4,000
Current assets		
Inventory	1,000	500
Receivables	1,100	700
Cash	200	500
	2,300	1,700
Total assets	9,300	5,700
Equity		
Share capital	150	150
Retained earnings	2,500	2,600
	2,650	2,750
Non-current liabilities		
Borrowing	5,500	2,500
Current liabilities		
Trade payables	1,150	450
Total liabilities	6,650	2,950
Total equity and liabilities	9,300	5,700

Statement of profit or loss

	20X1 £000	20X0 £000
Revenue	6,000	5,000
Cost of sales	4,500	3,000
Gross profit	1,500	2,000
Distribution and administration expenses	1,200	1,200
Operating profit	300	800
Finance cost	550	200
Profit before taxation	−250	600
Taxation	0	150
Profit for the year	−250	450

Complete the table below by calculating the key indicators (to 2 decimal places)

	20X1	20X0
Operating profit margin		
Interest cover		
Trade receivable collection period in days		
Trade payable payment period in days		
Inventory holding period in days		
Current ratio		
Gearing (debt/debt + equity)		

Write a brief note to explain whether Help Me Out plc is overtrading by stating the signs of overtrading and considering Help Me Out's performance indicators.

10 Overtrading

10.1 Overtrading

It is entirely possible for a profitable business to run short of cash. For example, a business may be making a profit but it has to replace a large item of machinery and this will deplete its cash resources to the extent that it may not be able to pay its payables when they fall due. In the worst case scenario this might even mean that the business is forced into liquidation.

It is also possible that a business may to be **Overtrading. Overtrading** usually occurs when a company tries to **expand too quickly** and **over-stretches its working capital** due to inadequate financing for its growth rate. If **sales increase too rapidly**, then working capital requirements may increase as **more money is tied up in inventories** of raw materials to support the increased sales levels; **receivables will also rise**. This can lead to a situation in which the company is operating at a profit but suffers a liquidity crisis as it has insufficient cash to pay its bills and expenses.

This problem happens over a period of time, with the working capital gradually being stretched and without the managers of the company realising what is happening as the company continues to be profitable. The statement of financial position eventually reveals the problem.

10.2 Identifying signs of overtrading

Through analysis of a set of accounts it may be possible to identify signs of overtrading as follows:

- sharply and rapidly increasing sales volumes

- falling profit margins despite increased sales as higher discounts are given to attract more customers and production costs increase due to overtime costs, etc

- greater reliance on short-term funding such as overdrafts

- longer receivable/payable collection ratios.

10.3 Controlling overtrading

Planned overtrading is not dangerous; it is the unmanaged and undetected overtrading that causes company downfalls.

If, however, the symptoms of unmanaged overtrading are detected, then the problem may be averted by:

- issuing new share capital or loan stock

- taking out long-term loans rather than overdrafts

- reducing the operating cycle by controlling receivables and payables

- slowing down the company's expansion.

10.4 Over-capitalisation

The opposite of overtrading is over-capitalisation. There is too much cash. Consequently profit is suppressed in relation to the capital investment in the company and earnings per £ of capital are low. If this surplus is not invested by the company to earn a good return, it could be distributed to shareholders through a higher dividend or a buyback of shares.

11 Credit terms and conditions

11.1 Introduction

Once a potential trade receivable has been analysed and it has been agreed that they can be offered credit then communication with them is required regarding a number of issues.

It will be necessary to request information from the new trade receivable to be able to **set up a credit account**. This includes:

- confirmation of name
- confirmation of address
- amount they want to be able to buy on credit
- VAT registration number

It is also necessary to agree the **terms and conditions** of the credit agreement (contract). Credit terms have to be drawn up for a company and must take into account the need to maintain both the company's cash flow and a sensible profit margin on the goods sold.

These terms must be **clearly understood** by the customer and it is sensible to print these clearly on the invoice to the customer. The company must be prepared to enforce the terms if the customer is late paying the debt.

🔍 Definitions

- **Credit limit** – the maximum value that may be outstanding.
- **Credit term** – the length of time amounts can be outstanding for.

When determining a credit limit it is necessary to consider the number and value of the orders the sales team expects during the credit term.

🔆 Example

The sales team expects weekly orders of £1,000.

The credit term is 30 days.

What would be a sensible credit limit?

If we assume that 4 weeks make up the 30 days than we would be prudent to set a credit limit of £4,000 to £5,000.

11.2 Types of credit terms

The most common types of credit term agreed between customer and supplier in the UK are as follows:

(a) **Cash with order** – This is effectively giving no credit, as no work on the order will happen until payment is received.

(b) **Cash before shipment** –This requires payment to be made before delivery and, while it safeguards cash receipts, if the customer refuses the goods at the last minute, a supplier could be left with bespoke articles which cannot easily be sold.

   Cash on delivery is much the same in principle but depends on a trustworthy driver to collect the payment and the customer to pay with a bona fide cheque.

(c) **Load over load** is an agreement to pay for the last load before the next delivery is made.

(d) **Net monthly** requires payment of one month's deliveries to be made by the end of the following month. It is not always possible to post invoices exactly to the correct month and so month-end deliveries may not be paid for two months!

   Net 30 days means payment 30 days after delivery and so brings forward the payment date on average 15 days earlier than a 'net monthly' agreement.

   Net 14 days brings forward payment to 14 days after delivery while **Net 60 days/Net 90 days** may be given if the market demands.

(e) **Stage-payments** allow for instalments of the expected total bill to be paid at agreed intervals. It is usual in certain trades (e.g. building and shipping) to make progress payments based on certified work during the course of the contract. Care needs to be taken when negotiating these terms and income matched with expenditure on the project; it is foolish to agree a down payment of 30% and the balance on completion if all the materials – constituting 70% of the final price – have to be paid for before the completion of the contract.

Whether the terms are agreed on a time basis as in (d) and (e) or on a delivery basis as in (a), (b) and (c), the terms must be clearly stated on the invoice and the accounting records must be able to identify customers who are late paying their debts.

11.3   A typical credit control policy and procedure

Credit terms and conditions should be laid out in a document which should be available to new and current trade receivables to review.

A typical credit control policy could be as follows:

New accounts

- One bank reference and two trade references are required.

- A credit reference agency report and the last three years published accounts for limited companies need to be analysed.

- A credit reference agency report and the last three years accounts for a sole trader need to be analysed.

Existing customers

- A credit reference agency report to be obtained on an annual basis together with the latest annual accounts (either from Companies' House or directly from the customer). Both documents to be reviewed.

- A trading history review to be undertaken annually to review for performance against credit limits and terms of payments.

- Annual review of usage of the customer's credit limit to ensure that an outdated credit limit is not in existence. This is particularly important where the trade with the customer has reduced over the past year.

Credit terms

- Standard terms are 30 days from invoice. Any extension to be authorised by the Finance Director.

- A 2% settlement discount to be offered to all accounts with a profit margin of 50% or greater, or with a profit margin of 30% and a value in excess of £50,000 or with the credit controllers discretion.

Debt collection process

- Invoices to be despatched on day of issue, (day of issue to be no more than 2 days after date of delivery).

- Statements to be despatched in the second week of the month.

- Aged trade receivable analysis to be produced and reviewed on a weekly basis.

- Reminder letter to be sent once an account is overdue.

- Telephone chaser for accounts 15 days overdue.

- Customer on stop list if no payment is received within 5 days of the telephone chaser. Computerised sales order processing system updated and automatic email sent to the customer contact and the account manager (sales person).

- Letter threatening legal action if payment not received within 30 days of the first letter.

- Legal proceedings/debt collection agency instructed subject to the approval of the Finance Director.

- Prepare a report suggesting an appropriate provision for irrecoverable or doubtful debts.

If at any stage in the process the customer is declared insolvent or bankrupt then contact the insolvency practitioner in order to register the debt and notify the financial accountant so that the VAT can be reclaimed.

Other things that would be discussed include:

- if there will be a **settlement discount** for prompt or early payment

- it will be necessary to agree how **payment** will be made

- **credit insurance**

- any **legal conditions** within the contract such as 'Retention of Title'.

11.4 Communication with trade receivables

There are a number of ways that a company can communicate with a trade receivable. Each method may be used as part of the set up checks or as an on-going method of managing trade receivables.

Face to Face communications are required:

- if there is a big contract being formed there is likely to be a face to face meeting to discuss and agree prices and payment schedule

- if there is a query over an invoice

- to confirm the existence of the company in question.

Telecommunications would include:

- telephone – telephone calls are a **quick way** of making personal contact and of obtaining an immediate response

- email – quick method of communication, can get delivery and read receipts on emails, good for audit trail of conversations

- internet – use to display credit control policy, any price changes.

Written communication would include:

- invoices – sent when goods/services delivered

- statements – sent once a month to show status of account

- letters – sent when needed i.e. to chase up payment, from solicitors etc.

Visits to trade receivables can be useful for:

- helpful in assessing their ability to pay

- in sorting out any administrative problems

- **establishing good relations** with key personnel.

Throughout all the communications with customers, it is important to remember that the **aim is to persuade them to pay their bill**. A firm approach is needed in all dealings to ensure this message is understood. Credit controllers should act with authority as late payment is in breach of the credit terms.

It is important that people with good interpersonal skills communicate with the customer to avoid unnecessary acrimony.

It is also important that pursuit of the customer is discreet and confidential. Broadcasting to the business community that a certain business is not paying its bills can have severe effects on that business, and may even result in libel writs.

12 Refusal of credit

12.1 Introduction

In some instances, after assessing a company, the credit manager may decide that it is not possible to trade with a new customer on credit terms.

12.2 Possible reasons for refusal of credit

The decision to refuse to grant credit to a new customer is a big decision for the credit manager as the business will not wish to lose this potential customer's business, but the credit manager will have taken a view that the risk of non-payment from the customer is too high for credit terms to be granted.

Refusal of credit does not necessarily mean that the potential customer's business is bad or is likely not to survive; it simply means that based on the evidence available to the credit manager the risk of non-payment is too high.

There are a variety of reasons why a credit manager may decide against granting of credit which include the following:

- a non-committal or poor bank reference

- poor trade references

- concerns about the validity of any trade references submitted

- adverse press comment about the potential customer

- poor credit agency report

- indications of business weakness from analysis of the financial statements

- lack of historical financial statements due to being a recently started company.

The credit manager will consider all of the evidence available about a potential customer and the reason for the refusal of credit may be due to a single factor noted above or a combination of factors.

12.3 Communication of refusal of credit

If credit is not to be granted to a potential customer then this must be communicated in a **tactful and diplomatic manner**. The **reasons** for the refusal of credit must be politely explained and any **future actions** required from the customer should also be made quite clear. The credit manager, whilst not wishing to grant credit to the customer at the current time, equally does not necessarily want to lose the business of this customer.

12.4 Trading on cash terms

In almost all cases where credit is to be refused to a customer, the company should make it quite clear that they would be happy to **trade with the customer on cash terms**. This may be acceptable to the customer, although not desirable, and the business will not be lost.

12.5 Future re-assessment of creditworthiness

In some cases, although the granting of credit to the new customer has been refused, it may be that the credit manager wishes to encourage the customer to **apply for credit terms in the future**. For example, with a newly formed company there may be little external information on which the credit manager can rely at the current time, but if financial statements and references can be provided in the future, then the decision as to whether or not to trade on credit terms can be re-assessed.

12.6　Telephone or letter?

In most cases it may be most appropriate to communicate the reasons for the **refusal of credit initially in a letter**. However, in such a letter the credit manager may suggest that a further telephone call might be appropriate in order to discuss the matter and any future actions that may be necessary.

> **Example**
>
> You are the credit manager for Howard Ltd and your name is Belinda Sean. You have recently been assessing requests for credit from three potential new customers.
>
> Kenwick Partners – they have requested to purchase goods from you, would like a £5,000 credit limit and 60 days' credit. You asked for trade references and bank references and financial statements for the last three years. They have provided you with a bank reference which states that 'the partnership appears to be well constituted but we cannot necessarily speak for your figures due to the length of time that the partnership has been in operation'. They have also provided one trade reference which is satisfactory from a company which allows Kenwick £2,000 of credit on 30-day terms. However, the partnership has only been in operation for nine months and therefore they have not been able to provide you with any financial statements.
>
> Fisher Ltd – this company has requested credit limit of £5,000 from your company and 30 days' credit. Two trade references have been provided (but no bank reference), along with the last set of published financial statements which include the previous years' comparative figures. The trade references appeared satisfactory although one is from Barnaby & Sons and it has been noted that the managing director of Fisher Ltd is Mr R Barnaby.
>
> Analysis of the financial statements has indicated a decrease in profitability during the last year, a high level of gearing and low liquidity ratios.
>
> Jacob Enterprises Ltd – this company is requesting 30 days of credit and a credit limit of £4,000. They have provided their statement of financial position at their year-end which was four months ago and the statement of profit or loss for the year to that date. The financial statements indicate fairly low levels of profitability but there is nothing to compare the figures to. The bank reference is satisfactory but of the two trade references one has only been trading with Jacob Enterprises for two months.
>
> You are to draft suitable letters to each potential customer.

Solution

HOWARD LTD
Dene Court
Dene Park
Hereford
HF3 9RT

Finance Director
Kenwick Partners
Kenwick House
Green Land
Watnall

Dear Sir

Re: Request for credit facilities

Thank you for your enquiry regarding the provision of credit facilities by us for £5,000 of credit on 60 day terms. We have taken up your trade and bank references which you kindly sent details of.

We have some concerns about offering credit at this early stage of your business as there are, as yet, no financial statements for your business that we can examine. Therefore, at this stage I am unable to confirm whether we can provide you with credit facilities.

We would of course be delighted to trade with you on cash terms until we have had an opportunity to examine your first year's trading figures. Therefore, please send us a copy of your first year financial statements when they are available and in the meantime contact us if you would like to start trading on a cash basis.

Thank you for your interest in our company.

Yours faithfully

Belinda Sean

Belinda Sean
Credit Manager

HOWARD LTD
Dene Court
Dene Park
Hereford
HF3 9RT

Finance Director
Fisher Ltd
Farm Road Industrial Park
Fordtown

Dear Sir

Re: Request for credit facilities

Thank you for your enquiry regarding the provision of credit facilities by us for £5,000 of credit on 30 day terms. We have taken up your trade references and examined your latest set of financial statements.

We are unfortunately concerned about your levels of profitability in the most recent year and also have some concerns about one of the trade references from Barnaby & Sons.

On balance we are not in a position to grant your request for trade credit at the current time, although we would of course be delighted to trade with you on a cash basis. If you do not wish to trade on this basis and would like to enquire about credit terms in the future then we would be delighted to examine your current year's financial statements when they are available.

Thank you for your interest in our company.

Yours faithfully

Belinda Sean

Belinda Sean
Credit Manager

HOWARD LTD
Dene Court
Dene Park
Hereford
HF3 9RT

Finance Director
Jacob Enterprises Ltd
White Hill
Blacktown

Dear Sir

Re: Request for credit facilities

Thank you for your enquiry regarding the provision of credit facilities by us for £4,000 of credit on 30 day terms. We have taken up your trade references and examined your latest set of financial statements.

We have some concerns about your level of profitability and would like the opportunity to examine your statement of financial position and statement of profit or loss for the two previous years. As one of your trade references has only been trading with you for two months, we would request details of a further supplier that we could contact for a trade reference.

At this stage I am unable to confirm whether we can provide you with a credit facility but will reconsider the situation when we receive your financial statements and additional trade reference.

Thank you for your interest in our company and in the meantime we would of course be delighted to trade with you on a cash terms basis.

Yours faithfully

Belinda Sean

Belinda Sean
Credit Manager

Activity 11

You are the credit manager for Style Ltd and your name is Henry H Oover. You have recently been assessing requests for credit from potential new customers.

NY Partners have requested to purchase goods from you, would like a £4,000 credit limit and 60 days' credit. You asked for trade references and bank references and financial statements for the last three years. They have provided you with a bank reference which states that 'the partnership appears to be well constituted but we cannot necessarily speak for your figures due to the length of time that the partnership has been in operation'. They have also provided one trade reference which is satisfactory from a company which allows NY Partners £2,000 of credit on 30-day terms. However, the partnership has only been in operation for nine months and therefore they have not been able to provide you with any financial statements.

You are to draft a suitable letter to this potential customer.

12.7 Trial period for credit

In some cases there may be some concerns about the information available about a potential new customer, but perhaps not enough of a concern to refuse to grant credit. In such circumstances it might be appropriate to **grant a degree of credit to the customer on a trial basis** with review of the situation at some point in the future.

For example, if a potential customer's trade references show that in one case although the customer has been given 30 days of credit they generally take 60 days to pay, then your company may offer them a fairly low credit limit on 30-day terms and monitor the situation for, say, six months when the situation will be re-assessed.

Example

You are again the credit manager for Howard Ltd and your name is Belinda Sean. You have been assessing the financial statements for Reed & Sons who have requested £6,000 of credit on 60-day terms. You also have received a satisfactory bank reference and trade references.

Your analysis of the 20X3 and 20X2 financial statements show the following picture:

	20X3	20X2
Gross profit margin	28%	30%
Net profit margin	4%	3%
Interest cover	1.5 times	0.9 times
Current ratio	1.3 times	0.8 times

You are to draft a suitable letter to Reed & Sons dealing with their request for credit facilities.

Solution

HOWARD LTD
Dene Court
Dene Park
Hereford
HF3 9RT

Finance Director
Reed & Sons
Ghyll Farm Development
Steel Cross

Dear Sir

Re: Request for credit facilities

Thank you for your enquiry regarding the provision of credit facilities by us for £6,000 of credit on 60 day terms. We have taken up your bank and trade references and examined your latest set of financial statements.

Although your references are satisfactory, we have some concerns about your profitability and liquidity. Clearly, your overall profitability and liquidity position have improved since 20X2 but their levels are still lower than we would normally accept in order to grant a credit facility.

However, due to your bank and trade references, we would be happy to offer you a credit facility for six months at the end of which period the movement on your account would be reviewed and the position re-assessed. The credit limit that we could offer you would initially be £2,000 and the payment terms would be strictly 30 days from the invoice date.

Thank you for your interest in our company and we look forward to trading with you on the basis set out above.

Yours sincerely

Belinda Sean

Belinda Sean
Credit Manager

13 Summary

In this chapter we have considered the question of whether to grant credit to a customer and how much credit to grant.

The decision as to whether to grant credit should be based upon external information such as references and also internal information created from ratio analysis of a customer's financial statements. After all of this information has been considered, a final decision can be made as to whether or not to grant the customer credit terms.

Answers to chapter activities

Activity 1

Answer B

Activity 2

Answer B

Activity 3

Answer A

Activity 4

Answer C

Activity 5

Answer B

Activity 6

Possible ratios – if you have calculated any others check with your tutor.

Return on capital employed	(570/3,500) × 100	= 16.3%
Operating profit margin	(570/6,000) × 100	= 9.5%
Current ratio	2,000/1,000	= 2
Quick ratio	1,100/1,000	= 1.1
Receivable days	(800/6,000) × 365	= 49 days
Payable days	(700/3,600) × 365	= 71 days
Inventory days	(900/3,600) × 365	= 91 days
Gearing ratio (total debt/total debt + equity	(1,500/3,500) × 100	= 42.9%
Interest cover	570/150	= 3.8 times

Activity 7

Operating profit margin

20X3	20X2
(53,500/525,000) × 100 = 10.19%	(41,000/425,000) × 100 = 9.65%

Interest cover

20X3	20X2
53,500/3,500 = 15.3 times	41,000/3,500 = 11.7 times

Current ratio

20X3	20X2
200,000/80,000 = 2.5	160,000/50,000 = 3.2

Gearing ratio

20X3	20X2
(50,000 + 15,000)/(325,000 + 50,000 + 15,000) × 100 = 16.67%	(50,000 + 5,000)/(205,000 + 50,000 + 5,000) × 100 = 21.15%

	Indicator	Rating	Indicator	Rating
Year	20X3		20X2	
Operating profit margin	10.19%	10	9.64%	5
Interest cover	15.3	10	11.7	10
Current ratio	2.5	10	3.2	10
Gearing	16.67%	20	21.15%	20
Total		50		45

Falcon Limited is very low risk and should be allowed credit terms

Activity 8

Jacket and Tie	Indicator 20X1	Indicator 20X2
Operating profit margin	13.6%	6.7%
Interest cover	9.5	3.1
Current ratio	2.7	3.3
Gearing (D/D+E)	24.6%	35.1%
Or Gearing (D/E)	32.6%	54.1%
Trade receivable days	65.5	66.5
Trade payable days	38.5	44.3

Workings for Indicators

Indicator	20X1	20X2
Operating profit margin	47,500/350,000 × 100	15,500/230,000 × 100
Interest cover	47,500/5,000	15,500/5,000
Current ratio	124,357/45,939	60,582/18,164
Gearing (D/D+E)	(15,000 + 21,959)/ (15,000 + 21,959 + 113,418) × 100	50,000/(50,000 + 92,418) × 100
Or Gearing (D/E)	(15,000 + 21,959)/ 113,418 × 100	50,000/92,418 × 100
Receivable days	62,789/350,000 × 365	41,918/230,000 × 365
Payable days	23,980/227,500 × 365	18,164/149,500 × 365

Note: The following answer is exhaustive you would not be required to cover all the points mentioned to gain all the marks available.

Jacket and Tie have been trading with us for a number of years and has always met terms until recently. The overall picture from the financial statements is that Jacket and Tie may be having a few problems financially as revenue and overall profit have declined significantly.

The operating profit margin and interest cover have both declined from 20X1 to 20X2. This is due to the decrease in sales revenue, which has dropped by 34% from X1 to X2. The cost of sales, the distribution and administrative costs have all remained approximately at the same proportion when compared to sales revenue. For example the cost of sales as a percentage of revenue in both X1 and X2 is 65%, the distribution costs as a percentage of revenue in X1 is 7% and X2 is 9%, the administration costs as a percentage of revenue in X1 is 14% and in X2 is 20%.

The current ratio has improved but when the SOFP is considered it can be seen that the cash position has declined significantly. This may be due to the company repaying the short term loan during 20X2 but it does not account for all of decrease in the cash.

The majority of the current assets in 20X2 are trade receivables, which are the least liquid of the current assets; this could be explained by the introduction of the new large clients as these are likely to be credit customers. There does not appear to be a problem with credit control. The receivables collection period has remained fairly static at around 66 days.

The trade payable payment period has increased and this ties in with their late payment of debts with us. The increase is not significant and once the new customers have started paying this may return to the 20X1 level as cash become more available.

The gearing ratio has increased but this can be explained by the introduction of a new long term loan to cover the purchase of the new non-current assets.

The company remains liquid and is maintaining adequate trade receivable and trade payable day ratios. If, as stated, revenue increases and variable costs are maintained then some improvement in these ratios should be seen.

If extension is to be granted I would recommend asking for some form of security, for example include a retention of title clause in the contract.

Activity 9

Sort Me Out Limited	Indicator	Rating	Indicator	Rating
Year	20X2		20X1	
Operating profit margin	−4.55%	−5	−6.92%	−5
Interest cover	0	−30	0	−30
Current ratio	0.96	−20	1.13	−10
Gearing	32.26%	10	13.33%	20
Total		−45		−25

Will we offer credit terms to Sort Me Out Limited?

No. Sort me Out Limited's credit scoring is high risk in 20X1 and moves to very high risk in 20X2. We could still trade with them but only on a cash basis.

Activity 10

Help Me Out plc	*20X1*	*20X0*
Operating profit margin	300/6,000 × 100 = 5.00%	800/5,000 × 100 = 16.00%
Interest cover	300/550 = 0.55 times	800/200 = 4.00 times
Trade receivable collection period in days	1,100/6,000 × 365 = 66.92 days	700/5,000 × 365 = 51.10 days
Trade payable payment period in days	1,150/4,500 × 365 = 93.28 days	450/3,000 × 365 = 54.75 days
Inventory holding period in days	1,000/4,500 × 365 = 81.11 days	500/3,000 × 365 = 60.83 days
Current ratio	2,300/1,150 = 2.00	1,700/450 = 3.78
Gearing (debt/debt + equity)	5,500/8,150 × 100 = 67.48%	2,500/5,250 × 100 = 47.62%

The signs of overtrading are as follows:

- Rapidly increasing sales revenue normally linked to extended credit terms

- Reduced gross and operating margins

- Increased inventory and trade receivables days
- Reduction in cash or an increase in overdraft
- Increased trade payable days

Help Me Out's performance indicators:

- Revenue has increased by 20%
- Operating profit margin has decreased
- Gross profit margin has also declined (20X1 = 25% and 20X0 = 40%)
- Inventory levels have increased by 100% from X0 to X1 and the holding period has increased by 20 days
- Trade receivables have increase by over 50% from X0 to X1 and the collection period has increased by about 16 days
- Cash has reduced but is still positive
- Trade payables have increased by over 150% and the payment period has almost doubled

It is possible that Help Me Out plc is overtrading.

Activity 11

Dear Sir

Re: Request for credit facilities

Thank you for your enquiry regarding the provision of credit facilities by us for £4,000 of credit on 60 day terms. We have taken up your trade and bank references which you kindly sent details of.

We have some concerns about offering credit at this early stage of your business as there are, as yet, no financial statements for your business that we can examine. Therefore, at this stage I am unable to confirm whether we can provide you with credit facilities.

We would of course be delighted to trade with you on cash terms until we have had an opportunity to examine your first year's trading figures. Therefore, please send us a copy of your first year financial statements when they are available and in the meantime contact us if you would like to start trading on a cash basis.

Thank you for your interest in our company.

Yours faithfully

14   Test your knowledge

Workbook Activity 12

A new customer, Crust Limited, has asked your company for credit terms. Your company has a policy of carrying out an analysis of a customer's financial statements as a part of an internal credit checking exercise, before deciding whether to agree to granting credit. Crust Limited has requested a credit limit of £30,000.

You have been given the financial statements of Crust Limited (extracts shown below)

Extracts of accounts of Crust Limited

	Current year £	Previous year £
Statement of profit and loss		
Revenue	3,100,000	3,350,000
Cash operating expenses	2,400,000	2,700,000
Operating profit	105,000	53,000
Finance cost	4,000	3,000
Statement of financial position		
Non-current assets	310,000	367,000
Current assets		
Inventory	62,000	66,000
Receivables	75,000	86,000
Cash and short-term investments	30,000	8,000
	167,000	160,000
Total assets	**477,000**	**527,000**
Equity		
Share capital	100,000	100,000
Retained earnings	225,000	260,000
Retained for the year	35,000	22,000
	360,000	382,000

Non-current liabilities		
Bank loans	40,000	30,000
Current liabilities		
Bank overdraft	5,000	28,000
Trade payables	70,000	75,000
Other payables	2,000	12,000
	77,000	115,000
Total equity and liability	**477,000**	**527,000**

Credit rating (scoring) system	Score
Operating profit margin	
losses	−5
less than 5%	0
5% and above but less than 10%	5
10% and above but less than 20%	10
more than 20%	20
Interest cover	
no cover	−30
less than 1	−20
more than 1 but less than 2	−10
more than 2 but less than 4	0
more than 4	10
Current ratio	
less than 1	−20
between 1 and 1.25	−10
between 1.25 and 1.5	0
above 1.5	10
Gearing (total debt/(total debt plus equity))	
less than 25%	20
25% and above but less than 50%	10
more than 50% less than 65%	0
between 65% and 75%	−20
between 75% and 80%	−40
above 80%	−100

Risk	Aggregate score
very low risk	Between 60 and 21
low risk	Between 20 and 1
medium risk	Between 0 and –24
high risk	Between –25 and –50
very high risk	Above –50

Using the template provided:

1   Calculate the key indicators for the current and previous years for Crust Limited.

2   Rate the company using the credit rating (scoring system) provided above.

Crust Limited	Indicator current year	Rating	Indicator previous year	Rating
Operating profit margin				
Interest cover				
Current ratio				
Gearing				
Total rating				

3   Based on your results recommend, with reasons, whether the requested credit limit should be given to Crust Limited.

4   If credit is being refused draft a letter to Crust Limited communicating the decision and explain what action the company could take to improve its chance of being granted credit in the future. If credit is being allowed prepare a telephone script which could be used by the person contacting the company to communicate the decision.

Workbook Activity 13

You work as a credit control manager for Trafford Limited which uses a credit rating system to assess the credit status of new and existing customers.

The credit rating (scoring) system table below is used to assess the risk of default by calculating key indicators (ratios), comparing them to the table and calculating an aggregate score.

Credit rating (scoring) system	Score
Gross profit margin	
losses	−6
less than 20%	−3
20% and above but less than 40%	0
40% or above	3
Current ratio	
Less than 0.75	−6
More than or equal to 0.75 but less than 1.25	−3
More than or equal to 1.25 but less than 1.75	0
1.75 or above	3
Credit rating (scoring) system	Score
Payable days	
90 days or above	−3
More than 60 but less than 90 days	0
More than 30 days but less than 60 days	3
Less than 30 days	6
Gearing (total debt/equity)	
less than 50%	3
more than or equal to 50% but less than 75%	0
more than or equal to 75% but less than 100%	−6
100% or above	−12

Risk	aggregate score
very low risk	Higher than 6
low risk	Between 6 and 1
medium risk	Between 0 and −7
high risk	Between −8 and −15
very high risk	Worse than −15

Existing customer requesting an increase in their credit limit

The sales department has asked for the credit limit of Alty Limited, an existing customer, to be extended from £50,000 to £100,000. The financial information below has been supplied by Alty Limited.

Statement of profit or loss	20X1	20X0
	£000	£000
Revenue	4,500	5,000
Cost of sales	2,750	2,000
Gross profit	1,750	3,000
Distribution costs	500	600
Administration costs	600	500
Operating profit	650	1,900
Finance cost	350	100
Profit before taxation	300	1,800
Tax	100	200
Profit for the year	200	1,600

Statement of financial position	20X1	20X0
	£000	£000
Non-current assets		
Property, plant and equipment	3,250	2,600
Current assets		
Inventory	400	300
Trade receivables	600	900
Cash	0	50
	1,000	1,250
Total assets	4,250	3,850
Equity		
Share capital	500	500
Retained earnings	1,700	1,500
	2,200	2,000
Non-current liabilities		
Loans	0	1,250
Current liabilities		
Trade payables	400	600
Overdraft	1,650	0
	2,050	600
Total equity and liabilities	4,250	3,850

New customer request form

The sales department has asked for a credit limit of £150,000 to be given to Hale Limited who is a potential new customer. The financial information below has been supplied by Hale Limited

Statement of profit or loss	20X1	20X0
	£000	£000
Revenue	10,000	9,500
Cost of sales	4,000	4,275
Gross profit	6,000	5,225
Distribution costs	1,100	1,000
Administration costs	2,000	1,500
Operating profit	2,900	2,725
Finance cost	700	600
Profit before taxation	2,200	2,125
Tax	200	200
Profit for the year	2,000	1,925
Statement of financial position	20X1	20X0
	£000	£000
Non-current assets		
Property, plant and equipment	7,250	4,400
Current assets		
Inventory	400	400
Trade receivables	750	700
Cash	100	400
	1,250	1,500
Total assets	8,500	5,900
Equity		
Share capital	1,000	1,000
Retained earnings	4,000	2,000
	5,000	3,000
Non-current liabilities		
Loans	2,500	2,000
Current liabilities		
Trade payables	1,000	900
Total equity and liabilities	8,500	5,900

Required:

Using the templates provided to one decimal place:

(i) Calculate the key indicators for 20X0 and 20X1 for Alty Limited and Hale Limited, and

(ii) Rate each company using the credit rating (scoring) system.

Based on the results of your credit rating, recommend, with reasons, whether the requested credit limits should be given to Alty Limited and Hale Limited.

Where the request for credit is being refused, draft a note or a letter communicating the decision and explaining what action the company could take to improve its chances of being accepted in the future.

Alty Limited	Indicator	Rating	Indicator	Rating
Year	20X1		20X0	
Gross profit margin %				
Current ratio				
Trade payables days				
Gearing %				
Total				

Hale Limited	Indicator	Rating	Indicator	Rating
Year	20X1		20X0	
Gross profit margin %				
Current ratio				
Trade payables days				
Gearing %				
Total				

Workbook Activity 14

Which of the following is not a reason for companies offering credit terms to their customers?

A   To reduce expenses

B   To increase sales

C   To improve cash flow

D   To improve customer relations

Collection of debts

3

Introduction

In this chapter we shall look at the cost of offering credit and the various methods of debt collection available.

ASSESSMENT CRITERIA	CONTENTS
Explain legal and administrative procedures for the collection of debts (3.1K)	1 Cost of offering credit
	2 Debt collection procedures
Evaluate a range of methods for the collection and management of debts (3.2K)	3 Factoring
	4 Invoice discounting
Select debt recovery methods appropriate to individual outstanding receivables (3.3S)	5 Credit insurance
	6 Restricting future trade
	7 Debt collection agencies
Explain the reasons for offering discounts for prompt payment and the effects on the organisation of offering such a discount (3.4S)	8 Settlement discounts
	9 Court procedures

1 Cost of offering credit

1.1 Introduction

There are a number of costs associated with offering credit terms to a customer:

- Finance cost.
- Non-payment of debts.
- Administrative costs.

The credit control team need to ensure that debts are collected promptly to ensure these costs are kept to a minimum.

1.2 Finance cost

The main cost to the company of granting trade credit is the **finance cost**. Trade receivables on the statement of financial position do not earn a return i.e. the cash is not in the company's bank account therefore it is not earning interest. This may lead to the company needing to raise extra finance to be able to pay bills e.g. use of an overdraft. A company that demands cash on delivery will have the cash available to pay bills so should not need to use an overdraft in the same manner. A company giving trade credit is effectively financing its trade receivable balances all year round in a similar manner to inventory balances.

> **Example**
>
> Z buys an item for £20 on 1 January 20X6 and pays the company one year later on 31 December 20X6. The company earns a profit of £4 on each unit sold. The company has an overdraft, paying interest at 10%.
>
> What profit does the company make from the sale of the unit after allowing for the cost of credit?
>
> **Solution**
>
> | | £ |
> |---|---|
> | Net profit on sale of one unit | 4 |
> | Less: Interest on overdraft | |
> | (£20 outstanding receipt × 10%) | (2) |
> | Real profit after credit period costs | 2 |

So the granting of one year's credit has reduced the company's profit margin by 50% which is a substantial cost to the company. A year's credit is longer than companies would grant but even a two month credit period costs a company a substantial percentage of the profit margin, i.e.:

	£
Net profit on sales	4.00
Less: Interest on overdraft	
(using simple interest) £20 × 10% × (2/12)	(0.33)
Real profit after credit period costs	3.67

i.e. (33p/400p) × 100% = 8.25% of the profit is lost.

In other words, it costs the company 8.25% to offer two months' credit to its customers.

If interest rates increase, then the cost of credit will also increase. The main board of directors needs to consider these facts when agreeing credit terms with the credit manager.

1.3 Non-payment of debts

A company granting trade credit may suffer **irrecoverable debts** as a customer may go out of business (go into liquidation) before paying what is due. This cannot happen to a company that does not offer credit to its customers as cash is required on delivery of the goods.

Definition

An **irrecoverable debt** is a debt which the credit manager is fairly certain will never be received from the customer.

An irrecoverable debt will **reduce the cash flow** of a business, as it represents **income which it will no longer receive.**

Definition

A **specific provision** for doubtful debts is a provision against a **particular** debt owed as there is concern than it may not be paid in full.

> ### Q Definition
>
> A **general provision** is a further provision consisting of normally a percentage of **remaining debts**. This reflects the fact that some debts may not be paid in full.

The specific and general provisions together form the doubtful debt provision which is credited in the statement of financial position against trade receivables, reducing the balance on the receivables. This provision is an accounting entry only and **does not represent any reduction in the cash flow.** It is a prudent thing to do to make sure the accounts are as accurate as possible.

1.4 Administrative costs

If a company does not give credit then the sales system will often be very simple to operate and hence cheap. A business giving credit, by contrast, has more expensive recording and collection systems, hence much **higher administrative expenses.**

2 Debt collection procedures

2.1 Administrative procedure

The collection of cash starts with the receipt of an **order**. The order is then agreed and processed. The business will deliver the goods and **send an invoice** detailing the payment amount and terms. It is helpful to file a **goods received note** in the credit management system as this helps credit controllers to substantiate claims of delivery. These notes must be diligently filed, having been signed by the recipient, dated and pre-numbered and matched with invoices. **Statements** should be sent out at the end of each period (usually monthly) detailing any outstanding balances. If the terms of the credit agreement are being met then **payment** will be received and this will be recorded in the accounts of the business.

2.2 Debt collection policy

Some customers do not pay their invoices promptly and a **polite reminder** may be needed. Some customers may require more than a gentle reminder; it may be necessary to take legal action to obtain payment.

It is important to have a **planned approach** to non-payment problems to ensure that the company's cash flow is not severely affected.

Each company will have its own version of the debt collect policy; below is an example:

Debt collection process

- Invoices to be despatched on day of issue, (day of issue to be no more than 2 days after date of delivery).

- Statements to be despatched in the second week of the month.

- Aged trade receivable analysis to be produced and reviewed on a weekly basis.

- Reminder letter to be sent once an account is overdue.

- Telephone chaser for accounts 15 days overdue.

- Customer on stop list if no payment is received within 5 days of the telephone chaser. Computerised sales order processing system updated and automatic email sent to the customer contact and the account manager (sales person).

- Letter threatening legal action if payment not received within 30 days of the first letter.

- Legal proceedings/debt collection agency instructed subject to the approval of the Finance Director.

- Prepare a report suggesting an appropriate provision for irrecoverable or doubtful debts.

If at any stage in the process the customer is declared insolvent or bankrupt then contact the insolvency practitioner in order to register the debt and notify the financial accountant so that the VAT can be reclaimed.

The length of follow-up period will depend on whether the customer has merely overlooked payment or is trying to extend credit terms further.

In most cases **with good credit control procedures monies will be received** from credit customers sometimes after encouragement such as reminder letters or telephone calls. However there will no doubt be some cases in which either the debt is never collected and has to be written off (irrecoverable debt) or the business has to resort to legal procedures to obtain payment.

Activity 1

Put the following in a sensible order for a debt collection policy

A   Send statement

B   Irrecoverable debt

C   Legal action letter

D   Issue invoice

E   Telephone call

F   Customer on stop

G   Provision for doubtful debt

H   Reminder letter

I   Start legal action

There are ways that a business can try to minimise the effect and, hopefully, incidences of non-payment or legal proceedings:

- Factoring
- Invoice discounting
- Credit insurance
- Restricting future trade
- Debt collection agencies
- Settlement discounts for prompt payment

3 Factoring

3.1   Factoring arrangements

Definition

Factoring involves the use of a factoring company to provide sales ledger services, finance and in some cases protection against irrecoverable debts in return for a fee.

A company may wish to outsource the collection of its debts through a factoring arrangement. This relieves the company of the burden of maintaining a detailed credit control system.

A factoring arrangement can be taken out with a factoring company (the 'factor'). Factoring companies are generally controlled by the clearing banks which gives considerable credence to the industry.

3.2 Options available

The factoring arrangement usually allows for the following.

(a) **Administration of the sales ledger and credit control functions**. The factor takes on the function of the credit control team. The factor will issue credit approval, chase debts and collect the cash. This facility only leaves the client the work of raising invoices and clearing disputes, as the factoring company effectively runs the sales ledger. The client has little need for a sophisticated computer system; the cost of such a scheme is between 0.75% and 3% of revenue.

(b) **Finance**. If the company requires cash immediately, the factoring company may provide up to 85% of the value of the debt immediately. This is effectively a cash advance and usually costs slightly more than bank borrowing rates. However, the payment is certain and allows for a determined cash flow.

(c) **Credit protection**. This can be provided by the factor to cover against irrecoverable debts. If the factoring agreement is 'without recourse' then the factor bears the risk of any trade receivables that do not pay. If the agreement is 'with recourse' then the customer will have to repay to the factor any monies advanced for the debt that is irrecoverable. 'Without recourse' is more expensive as the risk for the factor is higher.

3.3 The debt factoring procedure

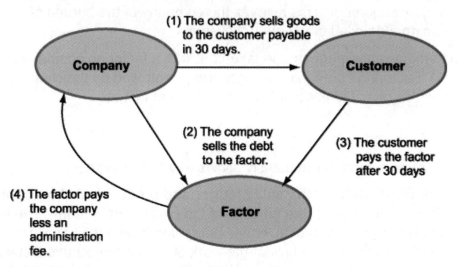

1   An invoice is raised as normal to the customer but at the same time the invoice/debt is sold to a Factor.

2   If the Factoring arrangement is being used to improve cash flow the Factor gives you up to 80% of the amount owing when the invoice is raised. If factoring is only being used to administer the credit control department this step is missed out.

3   The factoring company will make a charge for this service and then run the ledger and chase up the debts.

4   The balance on the debt is paid once the customer has settled with the Factor.

3.4 Advantages of debt factoring

Factoring is particularly useful in the early stages of development when a company is sufficiently large to need to devote attention to trade receivables but not yet large enough to warrant employing a full-time credit manager.

The advantages of debt factoring are as follows:

*   The company need **no longer incur the costs** of employing its own credit control staff.

*   Because the factor can act for several companies concurrently, the client will benefit from the **economies of scale** of such an organisation and the factor's fees are reduced.

*   The **cash flow advantages** that ensue from a regular predetermined cash inflow should reduce the company's financing charges thereby improving liquidity.

3.5 Disadvantages of debt factoring

The main disadvantages of factoring are that:

- Control of trade receivables is surrendered to the factor which may **displease customers.**

- There may be the impression the company is having liquidity problems.

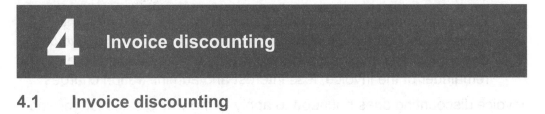

4 Invoice discounting

4.1 Invoice discounting

Invoice discounting is the purchase of invoices from a company, but, unlike debt factoring, the **invoice discounter does not take over control of debt collection**. The invoice discounter solely supplies an advance of cash.

4.2 The invoice discounting procedure

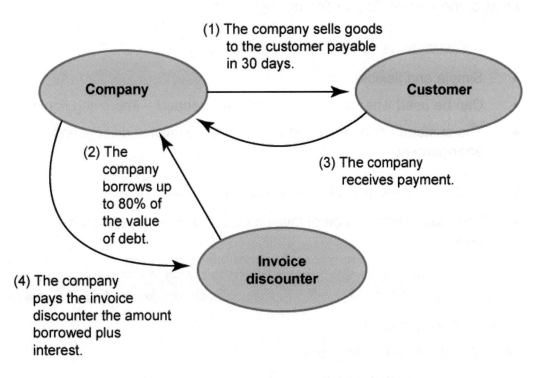

1   The company sends out invoices, statements and reminders in the normal way.

2   The invoice discounter provides cash to the company for a proportion of the value of the invoice, once it has receives a copy of the invoice and agreed to discount it. The discounter will advance cash up to 80% of face value.

3   The company then chases and collects the debts due from the customer.

4   When the company collects the payment from its customer, the money must be paid into a bank account controlled by the invoice discounter. The invoice discounter then pays the business the remainder of the invoice, less interest and administration charges.

Invoice discounting does not need to apply to the whole sales ledger and can be negotiated piecemeal for particular selections of invoices. When a batch of debts is assigned, the discounting company will advance up to 80% of the gross invoice value.

The invoice discounter relies on the credit control procedures of the business to get their money repaid. Therefore this service may only be available to well established companies. The customer does not need to know of the invoice discounting arrangement.

4.3   Advantages of invoice discounting

*   Simple and flexible.

*   Can be used when short term funds are needed – improving liquidity.

*   The customer does not need to know of the invoice discounting arrangement.

4.4   Disadvantages of invoice discounting

*   The main disadvantage of invoice discounting is the discounter's fees.

Activity 2

Invoice discounting is:

A   A reduced price for goods

B   A reduced price for early payment

C   A finance house lending money against invoices issued

D   A judgement by court

Activity 3

Bogstandard Brooms Ltd has been experiencing difficulty in collecting its debts within the terms of 30 days which they offer. Its sales ledger balances total, on average, £500,000 which is equivalent to 60 days sales. The company has an overdraft facility of £750,000 on which it pays interest of 8% per annum. Because of the high level of receivables, the overdraft level is never less than £500,000.

Cashrich Credit plc have offered them a without recourse factoring arrangement whereby they will administer the sales ledger, pay 85% of the invoice value immediately it is issued and the balance when they are paid by the customer or 60 days later, whichever is the earlier. They will charge 2½% of the revenue.

You estimate that this will save administration costs of the sales ledger of £15,000 per annum. Assuming that the customers will still pay after 60 days, will this be cost effective or not? Show your calculations.

Activity 4

A company has monthly credit sales of £200,000 and it gives customers 60 days credit. All customers take the full credit allowed. It has irrecoverable debts each year amounting to about 2.5% of revenue. It operates with a bank overdraft and pays interest at 8% on its overdraft balance.

The company's management is considering whether to use a factor to collect its debts, under a non-recourse factoring arrangement. A factor has indicated that it will take over the administration of the sales ledger and debt collection for a fee of 2% of annual credit sales revenue. This would save the company internal operating costs of £30,000 each year.

The factor would also charge 1.5% of revenue for credit insurance. The factor will advance 80% of the value of invoices as soon as they are sent out, and charge interest at 7.75%. If the services of the factor are used, it is anticipated that there will be no change in annual sales revenue and no change in the collection period of 60 days.

Required

Assess the financial consequences of using the factor for non-recourse factoring and factor finance.

5 Credit insurance

5.1 Credit insurance

Credit insurance is a method of **guarding against unexpected failures**. Credit management is still required but it is a way of safeguarding the cash flow. It may be particularly useful when a company deals with one or two major customers and is therefore dependent upon them.

Credit insurance is obtained through a broker who establishes terms and an agreement between the insured and the underwriter. The broker receives a commission for his work and, if he negotiates the policy well, will be able to renew it in the following year.

The types of cover available fall into four main categories:

(a)   whole revenue

(b)   datum line

(c)   catastrophe

(d)   specific account.

The amount that is usually claimed for is the **net** amount as VAT can be reclaimed from HMRC.

5.2 Selecting the correct policy

Each company will have its own system of credit control and its own pattern of sales/trade receivables. Entire revenue policies are available to cover all possible irrecoverable debts, usually with a de minimis limit, but these are often very expensive. A more specific policy can be taken out, such as a datum line policy, which covers customers whose indebtedness exceeds an agreed amount.

Alternatively, a policy-holder may decide to exclude certain large customers in whom he has full confidence and so the policy becomes quite specific in its nature with only certain individual accounts insured.

5.3 Terms of the policy

Most policies insure between 75% and 90% of agreed sales. The premium is negotiable between the parties.

A credit limit will need to be agreed for each customer. This is sometimes a difficult part to negotiate as the insured may well require a higher level of credit to cover the expected trade with the customer than the underwriter is prepared to accept. Trading above the agreed limit may invalidate the policy; but having to restrict sales to the customer may lose goodwill. A good relationship with the underwriter may help to solve this problem.

5.4 Pre-shipment insurance

Pre-shipment insurance is available to cover work-in-progress losses or losses of finished goods. It offers protection for orders cancelled at the last minute where there is no alternative buyer and only scrap value is obtainable.

5.5 Catastrophe policies

The main features of catastrophe policies are as follows:

(a)   the insured agrees to bear the first £1,000, say, of the loss due to the catastrophe

(b)   above this aggregate limit the cover will reimburse a specified percentage of the loss

(c)   this policy is not normally suitable for small companies.

Credit insurance is a means of **protecting against irrecoverable debts**; however, it is usually a **costly** way of obtaining security and many companies may decide to bear the cost of irrecoverable debts themselves when they are confident that this is less expensive than the insurance premium.

 Activity 5

Reign Ltd owes a balance of £48,000 including VAT. The account is on stop. Attempts to contact the customer by telephone and letter have been unsuccessful. The account is credit insured but only 75% of the value of debt is insured.

Complete the sentence:

Contact the credit insurer to make a claim for £_____, make a provision for £ _____and claim VAT of £_____ from HMRC.

6 Restricting future trade

6.1 Stopping supplies

Stopping supplies is one way of **preventing a problem escalating** with an overdue trade receivable. The credit manager must protect the company's investment and minimise the chance of an irrecoverable debt.

There are various reasons for non-payment of debts: the customer may be unable to pay, be inefficient, or be dissatisfied.

- If the customer is unable to pay, the supplier must safeguard his own position and ceasing to supply will prevent the debt increasing; however, the customer may claim he is able to trade out of the problem for which purpose he needs continuing supplies. The supplier needs to be quite convinced of this before releasing more goods.

- Inefficiencies may be quickly resolved by the prospect of a stoppage in supplies and this is often a useful jolt to rectify the position. If there is dissatisfaction over the supply of goods, however, stopping supplies is unlikely to resolve the problem.

- Customers who deliberately fail to pay need to be dropped from the sales ledger. Although there is often great reluctance to do this – particularly in small firms where there is a fear of losing business – it is the only answer.

6.2   Reducing credit limits and terms

The credit controller may wish to reduce the amount of credit a company can have and/or the length of time the credit balance is allowed to remain outstanding. This should then reduce the risk and enable the credit control team to take action before the issue becomes too serious.

7   Debt collection agencies

7.1   Debt collection agencies

A collection agency can be appointed to collect debts. Various types of agency exist but they can generally be split into three types:

(a)   **trade associations** are usually non-profit making bodies who charge an annual membership fee and a percentage of the monies recovered

(b)   **voucher agencies** sell books of collection vouchers to client companies who are entitled to complete a voucher for any outstanding debt and send it to the agency

(c)   **commercial agencies** usually work on a 'no-collection, no-charge' basis.

Collection agencies have the advantage of relieving the credit manager of the time-consuming work of chasing customers. A good agency will be specialised in tracing trade receivables who have disappeared, and will often have legal expertise. The charge is reasonable compared with the cost of employing another member of staff.

However, if the credit manager has good efficient staff they may be able to do the work and so save the costs of an agency. Customers rarely respond well to outside agencies whose sole aim is to obtain payment of a debt and goodwill can easily be lost by such steps. If a customer is regularly defaulting on payment then debt collection agencies can have more of a impact on the customer.

It is usually sensible to check that the agency:

(a)   is of good standing in the locality

(b)   is licensed for debt collection under the Consumer Credit Act 1974

(c)   is financially sound

(d)   uses an audited client trust account with its bank

(e)   reports regularly to the company and returns payments promptly.

 Activity 6

Debt collection agencies are used because:

A   They have extra powers to collect debts

B   The can stop other companies supplying goods to the trade receivable with the outstanding debt

C   They have the right to take goods from the trade receivable

D   Customers take more notice of them and are therefore more likely to pay

---

8   Settlement discounts

8.1   Cash or settlement discounts

With some credit agreements there will be a **discount offered** as an **incentive** to pay the money owed within a **certain time frame.** For example, the normal credit period may be 90 days, but the company may be prepared to offer a 1% discount for payment within 45 days. This would be described as '1/45, net 90'.

The costs and benefits of a cash discount scheme are summarised below:

Benefits	**Costs**
• Reduction in finance charges	• Cost of discount (reduced revenue received)
• Reduction in irrecoverable debts due to reduced collection period	• Extra administrative costs
• Improved customer relations and potential extra sales	• Potential abuse of scheme (customer takes discount but does not pay early)
• Improves short term liquidity as cash received sooner	

8.2 Assessing a proposed discount policy

There are two calculations that can be used to assess the annual equivalent cost of offering a discount either using simple interest or compound interest.

The simple annual cost of offering a discount to trade receivables is calculated by using this formula:

$$\frac{d}{100-d} \times \frac{365}{N-D} \times 100$$

Where: d = discount percentage given

  N = normal payment term

  D = discount payment term

Example – simple annual cost

Current credit terms are payment within 60 days. The finance director is considering introducing a settlement discount of 3% for payments received in the month that the sales invoice is raised.

Calculate the simple annual cost of the proposed discount.

$$\text{Annual cost} = \frac{d}{100-d} \times \frac{365}{N-D} \times 100$$

$$= \frac{3}{100-3} \times \frac{365}{60-30} \times 100 = 38\%$$

As it would cost 37.6% per annum to offer this discount, it would most certainly be cheaper to borrow from the bank to raise any funds required.

The **compound annual cost** of offering a discount to trade receivables is calculated by using this formula:

$$(1+\frac{d}{100-d})^{\wedge\,(\frac{365}{N-D})} -1)\times 100$$

Where: d = discount percentage given

N = normal payment term

D = discount payment term

^ = to the power of

💡 Example – Compound annual cost

Current credit terms are payment within 60 days. The finance director is considering introducing a settlement discount of 3% for payments received in the month that the sales invoice is raised.

Calculate the compound annual cost of the proposed discount.

$$\text{Annual cost} = (1+\frac{d}{100-d})^{\wedge\,(\frac{365}{N-D})} -1)\times 100$$

$$\text{Annual cost} = (1+\frac{3}{100-3})^{\wedge\,(\frac{365}{60-30})} -1)\times 100$$

$$= 44.86\%$$

As it would cost 44.86% per annum to offer this discount, it would most certainly be cheaper to borrow from the bank to raise any funds required.

✏️ Activity 7

What is the simple annual cost of giving a 5% prompt payment discount to customers who pay within 30 days rather than the usual 90 days?

A   21%

B   64%

C   32%

D   3.1%

Activity 8

A company is concerned about the size of its trade receivables and its cash flows. It therefore decides to offer a 'prompt payment discount' of 1.5% for payment within 14 days. Without the discount, customers take 60 days' credit.

What is the compound annual interest rate of the discount?

A   12.7%

B   39.1%

C   0.2%

D   39.7%

9 Court procedures

9.1   How to bring a dispute to court

If it is necessary to take legal action against a receivable who has not paid then the initial step is to instruct a solicitor. The solicitor will require the following:

- details of the goods or services provided
- the date the liability arose
- the exact name and trading status of the receivable
- any background information such as disputes in the past
- copies of any invoices that are unpaid.

In some cases there may be a negotiated settlement between the payable (money owed to) and receivable (money owed by) as the receivable does not want to run the risk of going to court. However in other situations the case will be taken to court.

9.2   Appropriate courts

Outstanding amounts owed to an entity are civil claims. Different courts and procedures will be followed depending on the value and complexity of the claim:

- Those with a value **under £5,000** will be dealt within the **County Court** under the **Small Claims Track** (sometimes known as the "Small Claims Court" although it is not a separate court).

- Claims **between £5,000 and £25,000** that are capable of being tried within one day are allocated to the **'Fast Track'** within the **County Court.**

- Claims **over £25,000** or more **complex cases** where the amount is less than £25,000 but will require more than one day in court are allocated to the **'Multi Track'** route. The multi track route will either be within the High or County court – depending on the Claimants choice of court and the nature of claim.

These 'tracks' are labels for the use of the court system not separate courts. A judge will decide if the case will be dealt with in a 'fast track' or 'multi-track' hearing once initial paperwork has been filed by the claimant and the defendant.

9.3 Procedure

The appropriate court, once it has received all of the paperwork will issue a summons to the receivable requiring an acknowledgement of service of the summons. If the receivable does not reply then the judgement will go against him. The receivable may admit the claim and perhaps offer to pay by instalments. If the payable does not accept this then the court will determine a suitable method of paying off the debt.

Activity 9

If an outstanding debt is more than £5,000 the court that would deal with any action would be:

A   The high court

B   An industrial tribunal

C   A small claims court

D   The county court

9.4 Enforcing a court judgement

Once the court order has been made then the money must be collected and there are a number of methods of achieving this.

(a) Garnishee order

A garnishee order allows the payable to be paid directly by a receivable of the offending company i.e., a third party who also owes the defaulting company money.

(b) **Warrant of execution**

Seizing goods is effective against businesses with valuable items in their offices, such as computers. The court bailiff is given a 'warrant of execution'. He will seize the goods and sell them by public auction with the proceeds paid to the payable.

(c) **Warrant of delivery**

A warrant of delivery is used by the bailiff to reclaim the specific goods that the outstanding debt is related to and return the goods to the lawful owner.

(d) **Attachment of earnings order**

An attachment of earnings order ensures that the payable is paid directly by the receivable's employer out of his/her pay packet.

This is only available against individual receivables who are in employment and is usually very unsuccessful as the court needs to determine the 'protected' earnings of the individual and the receivable's employer needs to co-operate fully. Such a person is likely to change employment frequently which creates further complications in tracing them and taking out fresh attachment orders.

(e) **Administrative order**

Where a receivable has a number of debts totalling less than £5,000 then the receivable might make regular payments into court and the court distributes them to the payables on a pro rata basis.

(f) **Charging order**

The court can order a charge on the receivable's property and if the debt is not paid within six months the payable has the right to have the property sold.

(f) **Bankruptcy notice** (against a partner or individual)

A bankruptcy notice is usually very effective as few people like to go out of business. For a bankruptcy order to succeed the debt must be in excess of £750, it must be unsecured and the receivable must be domiciled in the UK.

Activity 10

If payment of a debt is not forthcoming what action 'allows the payable to be paid directly by a receivable of the offending company'

A   Attachment of earning order

B   Garnishee order

C   Administrative order

D   Charging order

10 Summary

There are a variety of methods for collection of debts which may help businesses in different circumstances. Factoring arrangements can relieve a business of having to collect its own debts and can also be useful for cash flow purposes if funds are advanced and the debts are collected by the factor. Invoice discounting also allows money to be advanced to the business but still the business has the job of collecting their own debts. Debt insurance is a way of guarding against the non-payment of debts but is often a fairly expensive option. A collection agency can be used for collection of debts but this often has an adverse effect on the goodwill of the business. As a final resort a business can bring legal action to recover its debts, usually in the County Court or the High Court.

Answers to chapter activities

📝 Activity 1

Put the following in a sensible order for a debt collection policy

D	Issue invoice
A	Send statement
E	Telephone call
H	Reminder letter
F	Customer on stop
C	Legal action letter
G	Provision for doubtful debt
I	Start legal action
B	Irrecoverable debt

There are alternatives that would also be considered sensible e.g. the reminder letter may be sent before the telephone call is made, the provision for doubtful debt may be provided earlier in the process.

📝 Activity 2

Answer C

Activity 3

Currently the company is incurring two costs that could be saved if they accepted the without recourse facility offered by Cashrich Credit plc.

Savings

Admin costs of sales ledger	£15,000
Interest – 8% of £500,000 × 85%	£34,000
	£49,000

Costs

Revenue = 12 × (£500,000 ÷ 2)	£3,000,000
Charges – 2½% thereon	£75,000

As the costs exceed the savings, it would not be in the company's interest to accept the facility.

Activity 4

		Costs of factoring £	Savings £
Sales ledger administration	2% × £200,000 × 12	48,000	
Administration cost savings			30,000
Credit protection insurance	1.5% × £200,000 × 12	36,000	
Reduction in bad debt losses	2.5% × £200,000 × 12		60,000
Cost of factor finance	7.75% × 80% × £200,000 × 2 months	24,800	
Overdraft interest saved	8% × 80% × £200,000 × 2 months		25,600
Total		108,800	115,600
Net benefit from factoring	(115,600 – 108,800)		6,800

Activity 5

Contact the credit insurer to make a claim for (£48,000 ÷ 120 × 100) × 75% = £30,000, make a provision for £48,000 ÷ 120 × 100) × 25% = £10,000 and claim VAT of £48,000 ÷ 120 × 20 = £8,000 from HMRC.

Activity 6

Answer D

Activity 7

Answer C

The supplier gains 60 days' use of the amount due at a cost of 5%, i.e. an annual rate of:

(5/(100 − 5)) × (365/(90 − 30)) × 100 = 32%.

This discount rate is unlikely to be worthwhile in the UK.

Activity 8

Answer A

{ [(1 + 1.5/98.5) ^ (365/(60 − 16))] −1} × 100 = 12.7%

Activity 9

Answer D

Activity 10

Answer B

11 Test your knowledge

Workbook Activity 11

A company is concerned about the size of its trade receivables and its cash flows. It therefore decides to offer a 'prompt payment discount' of 3% for payment within 10 days. Without the discount, customers take 45 days' credit.

What is the amount the customer would pay on an invoice of £4,000 and what is the simple annual interest rate of the discount?

A   £3,880 and 112.9%

B   £3,880 and 18.8%

C   £3,880 and 32.3%

D   £3,880 and 310.0%

Workbook Activity 12

If payment of a debt is not forthcoming what action allows the business to be paid directly by the receivable's employer out of his/her pay packet:

A   Attachment of earning order

B   Garnishee order

C   Administrative order

D   Charging order

Managing trade receivables

4

Introduction

In this chapter, we will discuss liquidity and consider how it is best to monitor the trade receivables of a business, including how to communicate with trade receivables.

ASSESSMENT CRITERIA	CONTENTS
Evaluate a range of methods for the collection and management of debts (3.2K)	1 Liquidity
	2 Bankruptcy and liquidation
Explain the importance of liquidity management (4.1K)	3 Monitoring debt collection
Explain the effect on organisations following bankruptcy and insolvency of credit customers (4.2K)	4 Communication with trade receivables
Regularly analyse information relating to trade receivables' accounts (4.3S)	
Negotiate the payment of outstanding debts in a courteous and professional manger and record the outcome (4.4S)	
Promptly send information regarding significant outstanding amounts and potential irrecoverable debts to relevant individuals within the organisation (4.5S)	
Make recommendations to write off irrecoverable debts and make provisions for doubtful debts based upon a realistic analysis of all known factors (4.6S)	

1 Liquidity

1.1 Introduction

Liquidity is the measure of how much cash, liquid assets or assets that are easily converted into cash a business has. The main sources of liquidity are usually:

- cash in the bank

- short term investments that can be cashed in easily and quickly

- cash inflows from normal trading operations (cash sales and payments by receivables for credit sales)

- an overdraft facility or other ready source of extra borrowing.

Adequate liquidity is often a key factor in contributing to the success or failure of a business. Inventory and receivables need to be turned into cash to enable businesses to pay their debts (payables) and other expenses.

Liquidity in the business means **having enough cash** or ready access to cash **to meet all payment obligations when these fall due**.

1.2 What is cash?

The term **cash** is used to include bank accounts as well as coins and notes and cash payments include cheque payments, BACS, direct debits and standing orders.

1.3 The importance of liquidity

For many businesses their entire revenue is made on credit terms and therefore it is critical to manage the process of granting credit in order to ensure that sales are only made to organisations which will pay to terms and that timely collection of these amounts is taken.

Liquidity management is very important and effective credit control is a fundamental part of this.

Activity 1

Why is liquidity important?

A   To ensure that a company does not make a loss

B   So that the shareholders can see how much return they will get on their investment

C   So that the company can estimate how much cash is tied up in inventory and non-current assets

D   So that the company can ensure that cash is available to discharge commitments

2   Bankruptcy and liquidation

2.1   Introduction

Supplying goods or services to a customer is an **unsecured debt** and if the customer becomes insolvent then often little or no money will be received. There are different types of insolvency:

- **Bankruptcy** – applies to an **individual** or sole trader who cannot pay their debts (personal insolvency).

- **Liquidation** – applies to a **company** that cannot pay its debts (company insolvency).

2.2   Terminology

- The **Official Receiver** is an officer of the Court, a civil servant, who is appointed by the court once a bankruptcy order or winding up order has been issued by the Court.

- An **Insolvency Practitioner** is usually an accountant or solicitor who is in private practice. An Insolvency Practitioner is often appointed by the Official Receiver when there are significant assets involved in the bankruptcy or liquidation. An Insolvency Practitioner is regulated by the Insolvency Act 1986.

- **Secured creditors** – there are two types of secured creditors. Secured creditors with a **fixed** charge (i.e. a mortgage that refers to a specific asset or property) and secured creditors with a **floating** charge (i.e. a loan that refers to assets in general such as inventories).

- **Preferential creditors** – as defined by the Insolvency Act 1986 i.e. outstanding wages.

- **Unsecured creditors** – normal trade suppliers and the HMRC.

- **Administration** – is another mechanism for insolvent companies to allow them to carry on running their business. The process is an alternative to liquidation and in replacement of Administrative Receivership. Administration can be started by the **company, the directors, or a creditor**. A company in administration is operated by an **Administrator**. The Administrator takes over the running of the company (the directors lose their power) and tries to run it as a going concern while options to prevent liquidation are sought.

- **Receivership** – a company may be able to **avoid liquidation** by going into receivership. This is where a Receiver is appointed by **fixed charge holders** to manage the affairs of the company to try to regain outstanding monies owed to the business and also to pay off any debts owed.

- **Administrative Receivership** no longer exists under the Enterprise Act 2002 but they were appointed by a **floating charge holder**. They collected the debt from the company by recovering the property the debt was secured on. Technically Administrative Receivers can still be appointed, but only by floating charge holders, where the floating charge was created before 15 Sept 2003

2.3 Procedure for Bankruptcy and Liquidation

(a) The Court is petitioned by a creditor owed £750 or more.

(b) A Bankruptcy Order, or Winding Up Order (Liquidation) is issued by the Court. Any other legal proceedings relating to the receivable's property or debts are suspended.

(c) An Official Receiver is appointed. The official receiver takes control of the assets of the business and a statement of the assets and liabilities is drawn up – this is known as a statement of affairs.

(d) The Official Receiver summons a creditors meeting within 12 weeks of the bankruptcy order and may hand over to an Insolvency Practitioner.

(e) Assets are sold.

(f)   Distributions are made according to a strict priority:

- Fixed charge holders are paid first.

- Fees and charges of the bankruptcy or liquidation process.

- Preferential creditors.

- Floating charge holders (companies only).

- Unsecured creditors.

- The bankrupt, or company shareholders (if there is any surplus remaining).

2.4   Consequences of a bankruptcy or liquidation

As an unsecured creditor, the supplier is a long way down the list of payments and in a bankruptcy may not receive the money owed.

If a business does encounter one of its customers going bankrupt there are a couple of things that can be done:

- Invoke a **Retention of Title** clause, if present in the contract. This means the business maintains priority over any goods it has sold to the customer when the monies are distributed (see Chapter 1). The main problem with a Retention of Title clause is identification of the goods that have been sold. This will not work as well for a service provider or a seller of perishable goods.

- The business can claim **irrecoverable debt relief** (see Chapter 1). The VAT that has been paid by the business to HMRC can be recovered on debts that have gone bad.

✍ Activity 2

What is the correct order of distribution of assets if a bankruptcy order is issued:

A   Preferential creditors

B   Deferred creditors

C   Secured creditors

D   Unsecured creditors

E   The bankrupt

F   Bankruptcy costs

---

3 Monitoring debt collection

3.1 Introduction

As stated in 2.4, if a credit customer of a business goes into liquidation it is highly unlikely that the business will receive the cash owed. This will negatively impact on the cash flow of the business. Careful monitoring of credit customers is required to reduce the risk of this occurring.

The credit manager should closely monitor the collection of debts. Since this is of such fundamental importance to the cash flow, it is a regular if not daily task. It is important for all the departments in the company to pool their collective knowledge.

The credit manager needs to be looking for:

(a) customers who are building up a significant outstanding account

(b) customers who have not paid for a long period of time

(c) customers whose cheques have been dishonoured by their bank.

Any indication of the above should warn the credit manager that the customer may be having problems and he should warn the sales department to be wary of making any more sales to these customers.

3.2 Analysis of the aged trade receivables listing

The regular review of the aged trade receivable analysis should highlight the following potential problems:

* credit limit exceeded

* slow payers

* recent debts cleared but older outstanding amount

* old amounts outstanding and no current trading.

Each of these will be considered in turn.

3.3 Credit limited exceeded

If a customer's account balance shows that their credit limit has been exceeded then this must be investigated.

This is sometimes due to a **lack of communication** between the sales department and the sales ledger department. However, before a new sale on credit is agreed with a credit customer, it should be standard practice to ensure that this new sale will not mean that the customer has exceeded the agreed credit limit.

If a customer is highlighted in the aged trade receivable listing as having exceeded their credit limit then normally the customer should be told that **no further sales** will be made to them until at least some of the outstanding balances have been repaid. However, in some circumstances, liaison between the sales ledger and the sales department may result in an **increase in the customer's credit limit** if they have a good payment record and are simply increasing their trade with our company rather than just delaying payment of the amounts due.

3.4 Slow payers

Some businesses can be identified from the aged trade receivable listing as being slow payers as they always have amounts **outstanding for, say, 31 to 60 days and 61 to 90 days as well as current amounts**. In these cases consideration should be given to methods of encouraging the customer to pay earlier. This could be in the form of a letter from the finance director or perhaps more successfully the offer of a settlement discount for earlier payment.

3.5 Recent debts cleared but older outstanding amount

If a customer is generally a regular payer and the most recent debts have been cleared but there is still an outstanding older amount then this will normally indicate either a **query over the amount outstanding** or a problem with the recording of invoices, credit notes or payments received.

3.6 Old amounts outstanding and no current trading

This is probably the most concerning situation for a credit manager. In this case it would appear that the **trade receivable is no longer buying from the business** but still owes money from previous purchases. In this case the trade receivable should be contacted immediately and payment sought. If no contact can be made with the trade receivable or there is a genuine problem with payment, such as bankruptcy or liquidation, consideration should be given to writing off the debt as irrecoverable.

Specific provision for doubtful debts

As soon as there is a problem with a trade receivable which indicates they may be unable to pay a debt, it is **prudent to provide against the debt**. A specific provision can be set up for debts and a list is compiled of:

(a)   invoices disputed

(b)   invoices with warranty claims

(c)   part-payment invoices

(d)   old invoices

(e)   suspense account items.

The total figure forms part of the specific provision and is written off against the year's profit.

Assessing irrecoverable debts

The credit controller is in a position to be able to assess potential irrecoverable debts. Information used to do this might include the following:

- evidence of long outstanding debts from the aged debt analysis
- a one-off outstanding debt when more recent debts have been cleared
- correspondence with trade receivables
- outstanding older debts and no current business with the customer
- press comment
- information from the sales team.

Communicating potential irrecoverable debts

This will normally be the decision of a senior person in the accounting function. Therefore, if there is information about potential irrecoverable or doubtful debts then all of this information should be communicated clearly to the relevant person within the accounting function.

Incidence of irrecoverable debts

It can be argued that a high level of irrecoverable debts in an organisation is an indicator of poor credit control, although there could obviously be other reasons such as the general economic climate. A high level of irrecoverable debts could be an indication of:

- sales being made to high risk customers
- poor assessment of creditworthiness
- lack of useful information for checking on creditworthiness
- weak sales ledger accounting
- poor follow up procedures for outstanding debts.

Example

Wood Limited

Trade receivables' age analysis at 31.12.X1

Account no	Name	Credit limit £	Total £	Up to 30 days £	31–60 days £	61–90 days £	Over 90 days £
A001	ABC Limited	10,000	9,580	9,500	–	80	–
A002	DEF Limited	20,000	400	400	–	–	–
A003	GHI Limited	15,000	14,000	10,000	3,000	1,000	–
A004	JKL Limited	2,500	2,500	–	–	2,000	500
A005	MNO Limited	3,500	4,000	1,500	2,500	–	–
Total			30,480	21,400	5,500	3,080	500
%			100	70.2	18.0	10.2	1.6

Solution

Taking each trade receivable in turn we will consider what information the aged debt analysis has provided and what further action might be taken.

ABC Ltd   The vast majority of this debt is current therefore there may be some dispute over the £80 over 60 days old which should be investigated.

DEF Ltd   There would appear to be no problems with this account.

GHI Ltd   This would appear to be a slow payer and encouragement should be given to pay the older debts.

JKL Ltd   This trade receivable is a concern. There has been no trading with this customer in the last two months and their full credit limit has been used and is still outstanding after 61 and 90 days.

MNO Ltd   This trade receivable has been allowed to exceed the credit limit set by £500. The reason for this should be investigated and either supplies should be stopped until some of the outstanding balance has been cleared or the credit limit should be reassessed.

The percentage of each ageing of total trade receivables is also useful information for the credit manager as any increase in the older trade receivables percentage would be a cause for concern.

Activity 3

Jones Limited has sold goods on credit to Smith plc. The following information is available.

(i)   Aged trade receivable analysis

(ii)   Copies of outstanding invoices

(iii)   Copies of trade references

(iv)   Copies of contractual documents

(v)   Copies of bank references

Which of the above will be needed to aid collection of the debts from Smith plc?

A   All items

B   (i), (ii) and (iii) only

C   (i), (ii) and (iv) only

D   (iii) and (v) only

3.7   Updating the aged trade receivable analysis

The aged trade receivable analysis can be prepared by updating the previous analysis for any invoices issued in the period and any cash received in the period. The monthly balance, if still remaining unpaid, must then move into the column representing one month further outstanding. For example, if an invoice in the 'up to 30 days' column is not paid in the following month then it moves into the '31 to 60 days' column.

Example

Given below is an extract from the aged trade receivable analysis for a company at 30 April 20X4

Account	Name	Credit limit £	Total £	Up to 30 days £	31–60 days £	61 – 90 days £	> 90 days £
0001	Ace Partners	6,000	4,800	2,100 inv 0257	1,700 inv 0244	1,000 inv 0211	
0002	Aflek Ltd	10,000	8,850	4,550 inv 0259	4,000 inv 0247		300 inv 0196
0003	Amber Ltd	5,000	2,400	2,400 inv 0252			

During the month of May 20X4 the following transactions took place with these trade receivables:

Ace Partners	Invoice 0269 issued for £1,800
Paid invoice	0211
Aflek Ltd	Invoice 0266 issued for £1,300
	Paid half of invoice 0247
Amber Ltd	Invoice 0273 issued for £2,200

Update the aged trade receivable analysis to reflect the transactions in May 20X4.

Solution

Account	Name	Credit limit £	Total £	Up to 30 days £	31–60 days £	61 – 90 days £	> 90 days £
0001	Ace Partners	6,000	5,600	1,800 inv 0269	2,100 inv 0257	1,700 inv 0244	
0002	Aflek Ltd	10,000	8,150	1,300 inv 0266	4,550 inv 0259	2,000 inv 0247	300 inv 0196
0003	Amber Ltd	5,000	4,600	2,200 inv 0273	2,400 inv 0252		

Activity 4

You are working in Wilson Limited's credit control section. The Sales Manager has asked for your views on the credit status of four organisations to whom Wilson Limited supplies goods. Using the extracts from the aged analysis of trade receivables given below, analyse these four accounts and write a memorandum to the Sales Manager.

Your memorandum should:

- provide an opinion of the creditworthiness of the customer and the status of the account

- suggest how the account should be managed in future.

Customer name and address	Total due £	Current month £	Up to 30 days £	Up to 60 days £	Up to 90 days £	Over 90 days £
Megacorp plc Credit limit £85,000	72,540	10,000	11,250	12,250	15,500	23,540
Terms of sale: 60 days net						
Goodfellows Cycles Credit limit £50,000	24,000	9,500	9,500			5,000
Terms of sale: 30 days net						
Hooper-bikes Credit limit £25,000	26,750	5,000	6,250	4,875	5,275	5,350
Terms of sale: 60 days net						
Dynamo Cycles Credit limit £7,500	7,250	4,500	2,750			
Terms of sale: 30 days net						

MEMORANDUM

To: Sales Manager

Date: XX-XX-XX

From: Credit controller

Subject: Credit status of organisations

Activity 5

Task 1

An extract from EKAT's aged trade receivable analysis as at 30 April 20X7 is shown on the next page, followed by a proforma aged trade receivable analysis for May. You should assume the date is 3 June 20X7. Use the information below on transactions which took place during May to complete the May aged trade receivable analysis.

Customer	Information
Gartcosh	Paid invoice K449 £9,000.
	Invoice K496 remains unpaid.
	Invoice K521 £5,000 issued.
Strathaven	Paid invoice K495 £7,000.
	Invoice K511 £6,600 issued.
Coatbridge	Paid invoice K323 £3,000.
	Invoice K411 remains unpaid.
	Invoice K502 £2,775 issued.
New Mains	Invoices K289 £8,000 and K487
	£2,000 remains unpaid.
	Invoice K508 £4,000 issued.
Castlemilk	Paid invoice K442 £4,000.
	Invoice K472 £11,000 remains unpaid.
Rutherglen	Invoice K481 £1,000 remains unpaid.
Cambuslang	Invoice K204 £1,500 remains unpaid.
Easterhouse	Paid invoice K331 £10,000.
	Invoice K392 £13,000 remains unpaid.
	Invoice K510 £3,000 issued.
Airdrie	Paid half invoice K234, balance remains unpaid.
Stewartfield	Paid invoice K382 £3,000.
	Invoice K513 £5,000 issued.

EKAT Aged Trade receivables Analysis – 30 April 20X7. Credit terms: 30 days

Customer name and ref	Total amount	Invoice not yet due	Outstanding 1 month	Outstanding 2 months	Outstanding 3 months	Outstanding > 3 months	Action 1 Statement / 2 1st reminder / 3 2nd reminder / 4 Telephone call / 5 Warning letter / 6 Recovery action implemented					
							1	2	3	4	5	6
Gartcosh	£14,000		£5,000 K496	£9,000 K449			03-Mar K449 03-Apr K496	03-Apr K449				
Strathaven	£7,000		£7,000 K495				03-Apr K495					
Coatbridge	£6,000			£3,000 K411	£3,000 K323		03-Feb K323 03-Mar K422	03-Mar K323 03-Apr K411				
New Mains	£10,000		£2,000 K487			£8,000 K289	03-Jan K289 03-Apr K487	03-Feb K289	03-Mar K289	03-Apr K289		
Castlemilk	£15,000		£11,000 K472	£4,000 K442			03-Mar K442 03-Apr K472	03-Apr K442				
Rutherglen	£1,000		£1,000 K481				03-Apr K481					
Cambuslang	£1,500					£1,500 K204	03-Dec K204	03-Jan K204	03-Feb K204	03 Mar K204	03-Apr K204	
Easterhouse	£23,000		£13,000 K392	£10,000 K331			03-Feb K331 03-Apr K392	03-Mar K331				
Airdrie	£5,500				£5,500 K234		03-Feb K234	03-Mar K234	03-Apr K234			
Stewartfield	£3,000			£3,000 K382			03-Mar K382	03-Apr K382				
TOTALS	£86,000		£39,000	£29,000	£8,500	£9,500						

EKAT Aged Trade receivables Analysis – 30 April 20X7. Credit terms: 30 days

Customer name and ref	Total amount	Invoice not yet due	Outstanding 1 month	Outstanding 2 months	Outstanding 3 months	Outstanding > 3 months	1	2	3	4	5	6
Gartcosh												
Strathaven												
Coatbridge												
New Mains												
Castlemilk												
Rutherglen												
Cambuslang												
Easterhouse												
Airdrie												
Stewartfield												
TOTALS												

Action
1 Statement
2 1st reminder
3 2nd reminder
4 Telephone call
5 Warning letter
6 Recovery action implemented

Task 2

For the following customers, outline briefly how that account should be managed.

- Gartcosh   a medium-sized, regular customer
- Coatbridge   a large, major customer
- New Mains   a medium-sized, regular customer
- Cambuslang   a small and irregular customer
- Airdrie   a large and irregular customer

4 Communication with trade receivables

4.1 Introduction

This section provides examples of letters that could be produced to encourage payment of outstanding debts.

4.2 Collection letters

Collection letters are a quick and relatively easy way of contacting overdue trade receivables.

Each letter must convey the salient points, namely that:

- the trade receivable is late in paying
- the trade receivable is in breach of his credit terms
- payment is therefore due immediately.

A final reminder may be sent out if there is no response to the first. There is often little point in pursuing the trade receivable with many letters and sometimes a threat of legal action will result in prompt payment.

If further action is threatened, then the company must be prepared to carry out the threat whether it is to instruct solicitors, put the account out for collection or stop supplies. There are various letters that a credit controller may need to send out. These are described in the following sections.

4.3 First reminder letter

The first reminder letter is designed to **point out the facts**, the amount outstanding and as a reminder or encouragement to pay the amount due very soon. As with all letters to customers, it must be courteous and succinct as well as firm.

The first reminder letter will be sent out when the debts are a certain amount overdue. The timescale of the reminder letter will depend upon company policy towards debt collection but might be sent out 7 days after a debt becomes overdue. Therefore, if an invoice is sent to a customer with 30-day credit terms then the first reminder letter will be sent out 37 days after the invoice was sent out.

The first reminder letter will normally be sent to the person with day-to-day responsibility for payment of payables rather than more senior management.

An example of a first reminder letter is given below:

HOWARD LTD
Dene Court
Hereford
HF3 9RT

6 April 20X4
Accounts Payable Manager
Westrope Ltd
Account no: **021547**

Dear Sir

Further to our invoices detailed below, I do not appear to have received payment. I trust that this is an oversight and that you will arrange for immediate payment to be made. If you are withholding payment for any reason, please contact me urgently and I will be pleased to assist you.

Invoice no	Terms	Due date	Amount £

If you have already made payment please advise me and accept my apology for having troubled you.

Yours faithfully

Janet Bernard
Credit Control Manager

4.4 Final reminder letter

If there is no response from the initial reminder letter then there will tend to be little point in sending a second reminder letter. However, in some instances a telephone call at this stage is useful to clear up any misunderstanding and to assess whether further action is required.

The options for a company are to put the debt into the hands of a debt collector, to take the company to court for payment or to suspend any further sales to the company until payment is received. Whatever action the company decides to take, a final reminder letter must be sent to the customer detailing this action if payment is not received.

At this stage, the final reminder letter will normally be sent to a senior member of the management team such as the chief accountant or finance director.

An example of each type of final reminder letter is given below.

4.5 Debt collectors

HOWARD LTD
Dene Court
Hereford
HF3 9RT

12 April 20X4
Finance Director
Westrope Ltd
Account no: **021547**

Dear Sir

Further to our invoices detailed below and the reminder letter dated 6 April 20X4, I do not appear to have received payment. If you are withholding payment for any reason, please contact me urgently and I will be pleased to assist you.

Invoice no	Terms	Due date	Amount £

I regret that unless payment is received within the next seven days I will have no alternative but to put the collection of the amounts due into the hands of a third party. If you have already made the payment please advise me and accept my apology for having troubled you.

Yours faithfully

Janet Bernard
Credit Control Manager

4.6   Legal action

HOWARD LTD
Dene Court
Hereford
HF3 9RT

12 April 20X4
Finance Director
Westrope Ltd
Account no: **021547**
Total amount outstanding: **£2,279.50**

Dear Sir

Despite the previous reminders and telephone calls we have still not received your payment in settlement of the above account total. You have promised payment on a number of occasions but no payment has been received to date.

We regret that due to the above we have no alternative but to consider the Small Claim procedure in the County Court in order to recover the sum outstanding. Prior to us taking such action we would however wish to give you one final opportunity to make payment. We will therefore delay submission of the claim to the County Court for a period of seven days from the date of this letter in the hope that the account is settled. We will not enter into further correspondence regarding this matter other than through the County Court.

Please note that if we are forced to take legal action you may become liable for the costs of such action which, if successful, may affect your future credit rating.

Yours faithfully

Janet Bernard
Credit Control Manager

4.7 Stopping sales

HOWARD LTD
Dene Court
Hereford
HF3 9RT

Date: 12 April 20X4
Finance Director
Westrope Ltd
Account no: **021547**

Dear Sir

Further to our invoices detailed below, I do not appear to have received payment. I trust that this is an oversight and that you will arrange for immediate payment to be made. If you are withholding payment for any reason, please contact me urgently and I will be pleased to assist you.

Invoice no	Terms	Due date	Amount £

I regret that unless payment is received within the next seven days I will have no alternative but to stop any further sales on credit to you until the amount owing is cleared in full. If you have made payment please advise me and accept my apology for having troubled you.

Yours faithfully

Janet Bernard
Credit Control Manager

5 Summary

If an individual is made bankrupt or a company goes into liquidation, then the unsecured creditors are some of the last to be paid and may well receive only a small amount of that which is owed to them or possibly none at all. Careful monitoring of and regular communication with trade receivables should keep the risk of this occurring to a minimum.

Answers to chapter activities

Activity 1

Answer D

Activity 2

Answer C, F, A, D, B, E

Activity 3

Answer C

Activity 4

MEMORANDUM

To: Sales Manager

Date: XX-XX-XX

From: Credit controller

Subject: Credit status of organisations

Megacorp plc

Megacorp enjoys a high credit limit from our company. However the company is a poor payer and abuses the 60 days net terms of sale. Ways in which the account might be managed in the future include:

• The use of discounts for early payment or cash sale.

• Develop a better relationship with the customer to ensure prompt payment.

• Consider ways of providing a better service to Megacorp to facilitate prompt payment.

Goodfellows Cycles

Goodfellows enjoys a relatively high level of credit from our company, of which it does not make excessive use. It is a prompt payer, with the exception of £5,000 which has been outstanding for over 90 days. Ways in which the account might be managed in the future include:

- Settlement of the £5,000 due over 90 days. This possibly relates to a single item, on which there may be a customer query outstanding.

- Find ways of selling more goods to this customer.

- Develop better ways of managing customer queries.

Hooper-bikes

Hooper-bikes enjoys a medium sized credit limit from our company, which it has abused in recent months. Also it has exceeded its credit limit and urgent action needs to be taken to bring this account to order. Future action should include the following:

- Ensuring Hooper-bikes reduces outstanding amounts below the available credit limit.

- Considering reducing the credit limit.

- Considering ways of improving Hooper-bikes' payment record.

- Considering reducing sales to Hooper-bikes.

Dynamo Cycles

Dynamo Cycles enjoys only a modest credit limit from our company and has a good payment record. In the future we could consider the following:

- Increasing sales to Dynamo.

- Increasing Dynamo Cycles' credit limit.

Activity 5

Customer name and ref	Total amount	Invoice not yet due	Outstanding 1 month	Outstanding 2 months	Outstanding 3 months	Outstanding > 3 months	Action 1	2	3	4	5	6
							Statement					
							1st reminder					
							2nd reminder					
							Telephone call					
							Warning letter					
							Recovery action implemented					
							1	2	3	4	5	6
Gartcosh	£10,000	£5,000 K521		£5,000 K496			03-Apr K496	03-May K496				
Strathaven	£6,600	£6,600 K511										
Coatbridge	£5,775	£2,775 K502			£3,000 K411		03-Mar K411	03-Apr K411	03-May K411			
New Mains	£14,000	£4,000 K508		£2,000 K487		£8,000 K289	03-Jan K289 03-Apr K487	03-Feb K289 03-May K487	03-Mar K289	03-Apr K289	03-May K289	
Castlemilk	£11,000			£11,000 K472			03-Apr K472	03-May K472				
Rutherglen	£1,000			£1,000 K481			03-Apr K481	03-May K481				
Cambuslang	£1,500					£1,500 K204	03-Dec K204	03-Jan K204	03-Feb K204	03 Mar K204	03-Apr K204	05-May K204
Easterhouse	£13,000	£3,000 K510		£13,000 K392			03-Apr K392	03-May K392				
Airdrie	£2,750					£2,750 K234	03-Feb K234	03-Mar K234	03-Apr K234	03-May K234		
Stewartfield	£5,000	£5,000 K513										
TOTALS	£70,625	£26,375	£0	£32,000	£3,000	£12,250						

Task 2

Gartcosh

A good customer that appears to take over 60 days to make payment. Consider ways of encouraging prompt payment, e.g. settlement discounts.

Coatbridge

A large customer seemingly abusing their credit terms at the expense of a small supplier (EKAT). Consider ways of improving relationship and obtaining prompt payment, e.g. provision of settlement discount.

New Mains

A particular problem seems to exist with invoice K289 and invoice K487 is outstanding for two months. Establish whether a query exists with the invoice regarding quality or service. If there are no problems, consider ways of enforcing payment, using the legal process or a debt collection agency.

Cambuslang

A small customer with one outstanding invoice (K204). Establish whether this is in dispute. If not enforce payment using the legal process or a debt collection agency. Be prepared to write-off the debt.

Airdrie

Establish why K234 has been part-paid. Investigate why action has not been taken to recover this earlier. Negotiate with Airdrie for full payment.

6 Test your knowledge

Workbook Activity 6

What is the correct order of distribution of assets if a liquidation order is issued:

A   Preferential creditors

B   Shareholders

C   Secured creditors

D   Unsecured creditors

E   Holders of floating charges

F   Liquidation costs

Workbook Activity 7

Debt collection policy for Green Ltd is as follows:

(i)   Invoices are issued at time of delivery.

(ii)   Statements are sent monthly.

(iii)   Terms are payment within 30 days.

(iv)   Aged analysis is produced monthly.

(v)   Reminder letter is sent when debt is 14 days overdue.

(vi)   At 28 days overdue a telephone call is made and account is put on stop.

(vii) At 60 days overdue it is placed in hands of debt collector unless debt is disputed.

(viii) At 90 days overdue legal proceedings are started.

Aged analysis of trade receivables at 31 March 2010

Customer	Balance £	Current £	31–60 days £	61–90 days £	Over 90 days £
White Ltd	32,000				32,000
Grey Ltd	24,800		24,800		
Brown Ltd	144,000			48,000	96,000

Notes

- White Ltd went into liquidation a little while ago and the statement of affairs shows that there are very few assets.

- Grey Ltd is a regular customer and the latest invoice is dated 28 February 2010.

- Brown Ltd has historically been a good payer, but there are rumours that the business is currently in trouble due to overtrading.

For each of the above, state what action should have been taken to date, and what further action will be taken. State whether any provision should be made in each case

Workbook Activity 8

Debt collection policy for Purple Ltd is as follows:

(i)   Invoices are issued at time of delivery.

(ii)   Terms are payment within 30 days.

(iii)   Aged analysis is produced monthly.

(iv)   Reminder telephone call is made when the debt is 7 days overdue.

(v)   Overdue letter is sent when debt is 14 days overdue.

(vi)   At 28 days overdue the account is put on stop.

(vii) At 60 days overdue it is placed in hands of debt collector unless debt is disputed or legal proceedings are started.

(viii) Purple is credit insured, however insurance is only given for customers once they have a history of trade with the business of at least 12 months and have successfully paid at least 2 invoiced amounts.

Aged analysis of trade receivables at 31 October 2010

Customer	Balance £	Current £	31–60 days £	61–90 days £	Over 90 days £
Orange Ltd	40,000				40,000
Yellow Ltd	22,500		22,500		
Red Ltd	50,000			24,000	26,000

Notes

*   Orange Ltd is a new customer and has said that the goods were not received in good condition. The delivery note states that any claim for poor quality goods has to be notified to Purple Ltd within 24 hours. Orange Limited only raised a problem with the goods when they were called for a second time. They did not mention that the goods were poor quality on the first call or within 24 hours of delivery.

*   Yellow Ltd is a regular customer and usually pays to terms.

*   Red Ltd is refusing to pay even though there is no dispute.

For each of the above, state what action should have been taken to date and what further action will need to be taken. State whether any provision should be made in each case.

Workbook Activity 9

You work for Henry Tudor. The policy for the collection of debts, an extract from the aged receivables analysis and supporting customer notes are set out below. You should assume that today's date is 1 October 20Y0. On the basis of this information, write a memo to Henry Tudor. Your memo should include:

1 In the case of Francis Ltd, a note of the matters to be discussed by telephone

2 In the case of Nicholas Evans, who is a sole trader, a description of two methods which may be used to enforce judgement

3 The credit control action required for each of the other accounts.

Debt collection policy

1   Invoices must be issued on the same day as goods are despatched.

2   An aged analysis of trade receivables is to be produced monthly.

3   Statements are to be despatched on the first working day of each month.

4   A reminder letter must be sent when a debt is 7 days overdue.

5   A telephone call to chase payment must be made when a debt is 14 days overdue.

6   The customer will be placed on the stop list when the debt is 30 days overdue and a meeting arranged with the customer to discuss the operation of the account.

7   When the debt is 45 days overdue it will be placed in the hands of a debt collector. At this stage, consideration must be given as to whether to provide for the outstanding debt.

8   Legal proceedings are to be commenced when a debt is 90 days overdue subject to agreement with the Financial Controller.

Aged receivable analysis at 30 September 20Y0

Customer	Amount due £	Current £	31–60 Days £	61 – 90 days £	91+ days £
Francis Ltd	8,500		8,500		
Nicholas Evans	3,700				3,700
Shields	1,300	550		750	
Outdoors	850			850	

Notes

1   All four accounts were offered 30 day credit terms.

2   There are two outstanding invoices from Francis Ltd, both dated 16 August 20Y0.

3   A county court judgement has been obtained against Nicholas Evans.

4   There is an outstanding invoice from Shields Ltd for £750 dated 25 July 20Y0.

5   The amount due from Outdoors Ltd relates to an invoice dated 5 July 20Y0.

Memorandum

WORKBOOK ACTIVITIES
ANSWERS

Workbook activities answers

1 Legislation

Activity 11

No – the additional amount does not have to be paid as the agreement was for £300.

Activity 12

Answer B

2 Granting credit

Activity 12

Crust Limited	Indicator current year	Rating	Indicator previous year	Rating
Operating profit margin	3.4%	0	1.6%	0
Interest cover	26.3	10	17.7	10
Current ratio	2.2	10	1.4	0
Gearing	11.11%	20	13.18%	20
Total rating		40		30

Workings for Indicators

Indicator	Current year	Previous year
Operating profit margin	105,000/3,100,000 × 100	53,000/3,350,000 × 100
Interest cover	105,000/4,000	53,000/3,000
Current ratio	167,000/77,000	160,000/115,000
Gearing	40,000 + 5,000/(360,000 + 40,000 + 5,000) × 100	30,000 + 28,000/(382,000 + 30,000 + 28,000) × 100

Crust Limited is a very low risk for both sets of accounts analysed.

Draft notes for telephone call:

Ensure that conversation is with the relevant person.

Confirm that credit will be granted.

Request the information to be able to set up a credit account. This includes:

- confirmation of name
- confirmation of address
- VAT registration number.

It is also necessary to agree the terms and conditions of the credit agreement i.e. confirm credit terms and credit limit.

Other things that would be discussed include:

- if there will be a settlement discount for prompt or early payment
- it will be necessary to agreeing how payment will be
- any legal conditions within the contract such as 'Retention of Title'.

Activity 13

Alty Limited	Indicator	Rating	Indicator	Rating
Year	20X1		20X0	
Gross profit margin %	38.89	0	60.00	3
Current ratio	0.49	–6	2.08	3
Trade payables days	53.09	3	109.50	–3
Gearing %	75.00	–6	62.50	0
		–9		3

Workings – Alty	Indicator	Indicator
Year	20X1	20X0
Gross profit margin %	1,750/4,500 × 100	3,000/5,000 × 100
Current ratio	1,000/2,050	1,250/600
Trade payables days	400/2,750 × 365	600/2,000 × 365
Gearing %	(1,650 + 0)/2,200 × 100	(0 + 1,250)/2,000 × 100

Hale Limited	Indicator	Rating	Indicator	Rating
Year	20X1		20X0	
Gross profit margin %	60.00	3	55.00	3
Current ratio	1.25	0	1.67	0
Trade payables days	91.25	–3	76.84	0
Gearing %	50.00	0	67.00	0
		0		3

Workings – Hale	Indicator	Indicator
Year	20X1	20X0
Gross profit margin %	6,000/10,000 × 100	5,225/9,500 × 100
Current ratio	1,250/1,000	1,500/900
Trade payables days	1,000/4,000 ×	900/4,275 × 365
Gearing %	2,500/5,000 × 100	2,000/3,000 × 100

Alty Limited

- Alty was rated as low risk (borderline very low risk) in 20X0 explaining why credit was given.

- Alty has been impacted by the credit crunch, with declining revenue and rising costs in the Statement of profit or loss.

- The credit crunch has also impacted on Alty's ability to re-finance the long term loan, resulting in the company being financed via an overdraft which is repayable on demand and considerably more expensive (evidenced by the increased finance cost in the Statement of profit or loss).

Alty is now rated as high risk suggesting that credit should be refused. In addition it is recommended that the current credit limit is reviewed with the following possible options:

- Remove the credit facility.

- Reduce the current credit limit to a much lower level.

- Possibly insist on retention of title clauses.

Recommendation:

- The credit limit should be reduced over the next few months until Alty can convince us that it has put in place steps to control its cost base and refinance the long term loan.

- If Alty fails to do this over the next few months, the credit facility should be removed.

Hale Limited

- Hale is rated as medium risk indicating that the credit request should also be refused, however, this decision is a marginal one. The score of 0 being on the border between low and medium risk.

- In addition in the prior year Hale's score was in the low risk area and during the year trading results and profit have improved, as has the gearing of the company.

- The main reason for the decline in score is the increase in trade payables days. Therefore the following possible options exist:

- Refuse credit.

- Offer a lower credit limit than the £150,000 proposed.

Recommendation:

- An initial lower credit limit should be granted (£50,000, for example). Hale Limited should be encouraged to reduce their payables days before any increase is proposed.

- If trade payables days improve then further credit up to the £150,000 can be offered.

Refusal of credit – Alty Limited

Introduction:

- Increase refused due to concerns regarding refinancing of long term loan and the impact of the credit crunch on business.

- Credit limit will be reduced over the next few months until refinancing has occurred.

- Action points for Alty to improve liquidity:

- Re-finance overdraft (as a long term loan) to reduce finance cost, and current ratio.

- Look at cost base to try to improve margins.

- Consider raising some equity finance to reduce gearing.

Other recommendations:

- Possibly insist on retention of title clauses.

Refusal to raise limit – Hale Limited

Introduction:

- £150,000 credit limit refused, however an initial smaller credit limit will be offered for example £50,000.

- Credit limit will be increased as Hale demonstrates prompt payment of amounts owing.

- Action points for Hale to improve creditworthiness:

- Improve payment speed to trade payables.

Activity 14

Answer A

3 Collection of debts

Activity 11

Answer C

£4,000 × 97% = £3,880

(3/97) × (365/(45 − 10)) × 100 = 32.3%

Activity 12

Answer A

4 Managing trade receivables

Activity 6

Answer C, F, A, E, D, B

Activity 7

Receivable	Completed action	Further action
White	All action should have been taken.	As unsecured receivables are low down the list when paying in a case of liquidation – write off the debt (irrecoverable debt).
Grey	Should have received invoice and statement.	No further action required at this stage as the debt is not yet 14 days overdue.

| Brown | Both amounts should have been placed in the hands of a debt collector. Legal proceeding should have started for the £96,000 debt. | Provision for doubtful debt as there is doubt over whether the company is going to be able to keep trading. |

Activity 8

Receivable	Completed action	Further action
Orange	All above action should have been taken.	Orange is in breach of contract as they had not contacted Purple within the agreed timescales. Purple can take Orange to court to seek action for damages etc. It is not possible to use the credit insurance as Orange is a new customer. Provision should be made.
Yellow	Invoice and statement should have been sent.	Reminder telephone call may be required depending on the date of the invoice.
Red	All above action should have been taken.	Both debts need to be placed in the hands of the debt collector – there is no dispute. Credit insurance may be possible but more detail is required about length of trading. Provision should be made.

Activity 9

Memorandum

To: Henry Tudor

From: AAT Student

Date: 1 October 20Y0

Subject: Monitoring and collection of debts

Francis Ltd – only 14 days overdue as invoice is dated 16 August and each invoice has 30 day credit term. A telephone call is needed to discuss payment of debt. Matters to note:

- Remain polite and courteous.
- Debt of £8,500 is now overdue.
- Is there any query with the invoice?
- If not when will money be received?

Nicholas Evans – county court judgement has been attained. Methods to enforce this judgement include:

- Warrant of execution.
- Warrant of delivery.
- Garnishee order.
- Charging order.
- Bankruptcy notice.

Shields Ltd – debt is 30 days overdue. Account put on stop and a meeting needs to be arranged.

Outdoors Ltd – debt is more than 45 days overdue. Debt needs to be placed in the hands of a debt collector. Make a provision for this debt.

MOCK ASSESSMENT

1 Mock Assessment Questions

Task 1

(a) The essential features of a valid simple contract are:

    A   Offer, acceptance and consideration only

    B   Offer, acceptance, consideration, intention to create legal relations and certainty of terms only

    C   Offer and acceptance only

    D   Offer, acceptance and intention to create legal relations only

(b) Steve orders a takeaway by telephone and says he will pay on delivery. Which of the following would constitute consideration?

    A   Calling the restaurant

    B   Handing over money to the delivery person

    C   Accepting delivery of the takeaway

    D   Promising to pay for the takeaway

(c) Tina is the owner of a florist. She places a notice in the window advertising the sale of roses at half price. The notice is:

    A   A contractual offer

    B   A completed contract

    C   An acceptance of an offer

    D   An invitation to treat

(d) Jack receives a letter from Mark containing an order of 50 kg of sugar for £100. Which of the following statements is correct?

    A   Mark's letter is an invitation to treat and Jack's response that he can supply the sugar is an offer

    B   Mark's letter is an offer and Jack's response that he can supply the sugar is an acceptance

    C   Mark's letter is an acceptance and Jack's response that he cannot supply the sugar is a breach of contract

    D   Mark's letter is an acceptance and Jack's response that he can supply the sugar is consideration

(e) The normal remedy for breach of contract due to non payment of the debt is:

A An action for specific performance

B An action for price

C An action for remedy

D An action for the goods

(f) Retention of title is:

A The right of the purchaser to retain ownership of the goods received

B The right of the seller to retain ownership of the goods until a cheque has been posted

C The right of the seller to retain ownership of the goods until payment is made

D The right of the purchaser to expect that title is retained by the seller even when payment has been received

(g) Legal action can be taken against a customer for non payment of an invoice when:

A There is a contract in existence and the non payment is a breach of contract

B There is no contract in existence but the payment is still due

C There is a contract in existence and the non payment is a misrepresentation

D There is a contract in existence and the non payment is a remedy

(h) A customer owes £6,000 excluding VAT and the debt is 90 days late. The current Bank of England base rate is 1.5%. Calculate the interest charge under the Late Payment of Commercial Debts (interest) Act to the nearest penny.

The interest charge will be £_____

(i) The Data Protection Act applies to:

A Data about individuals only

B Data about individuals, companies and government departments

C Data about companies only

D Data about individuals and companies only

Task 2

(a) Why is liquidity management important?

    A   Liquidity management is important to ensure that a company does not make a loss

    B   Liquidity management is important so that the shareholders can see how much return they will get on their investment

    C   Liquidity management is important so that the company can estimate how much cash is tied up in inventory and fixed assets

    D   Liquidity management is important so that the company can ensure that cash is available to discharge commitments

(b) In order to petition the court for a winding up order, the company must be owed at least:

    A   £75

    B   £750

    C   £7,500

    D   £1,000

(c) Ben has sold goods on credit to Jerry Limited. The following information is available.

    (i)   Aged trade receivable analysis

    (ii)   Copies of outstanding invoices

    (iii)   Copies of contractual documents

    (iv)   Copies of trade references

    (v)   Copies of bank references

Which of the above documents will be needed to aid the collection of the outstanding amounts owed by Jerry Limited?

    A   All items

    B   (i), (ii) and (iii) only

    C   (i), (iv) and (v) only

    D   (iv) and (v) only

(d) A company's terms of payment are 30 days. It is offering a discount of 4% for payment within 15 days. Calculate the simple annual interest rate of the discount.

    A   58.402%

    B   97.33%

    C   101.39%

    D   17.12%

(e) Credit insurance allows a company to claim for:

    A   Amounts owed by a customer who has defaulted on payment

    B   Amounts owed to a bank on a mortgage

    C   Amounts owed to payables when a company makes losses

    D   Amounts owed to shareholders when a director has acted illegally

(f) Organisations often use debt collection agencies because:

    A   Debt collection agencies have more powers than ordinary companies

    B   Debt collection agencies can place customers on stop with all other suppliers in the sector

    C   Debt collection agencies have a right to seize goods from customer

    D   Debt collection agencies get results because customers take more notice and are more likely to pay

(g) Ben has a customer, Jerry Limited, who refuses to pay an outstanding amount of £500. Which of the following will deal with any action taken by Ben to enforce the repayment of the debt?

    A   The High Court

    B   Multi track

    C   Small claims track

    D   Fast track

(h)   Ben has been trading with Jerry for many years. Jerry purchased
       5,500 units of a product prices at £8 per unit including VAT. At the
       31 December 20X4 Jerry owed Ben £2,600.

       The receivable collection period in days for the amount owing by
       Jerry is _____ days

(i)   Ben is looking to improve his cash flow and has been considering
       various finance products. Ben has forecast sales of £54,000 for the
       following year.

       A finance company has offered to provide a facility where Ben can
       be advanced 80% of his invoiced sales. The finance company will
       not administer the sales ledger.

       Ben can borrow £_____. This is an example of:

       A   Factoring

       B   Credit insurance

       C   Invoice discounting

       D   Settlement discounting

Task 3

You work as a credit control manager for Lamb Limited which uses a credit rating system to assess the credit status of new customers.

The credit rating (scoring) system table below is used to assess the risk of default by calculating key indicators (ratios), comparing them to the table and calculating an aggregate score.

Credit rating (scoring) system	Score	Credit rating (scoring) system	Score
Operating profit margin		**Current ratio**	
Losses	–5	Less than 1	–20
Less than 5%	0	Between 1 and 1.25	–10
5% and above but less than 10%	5	Between 1.25 and 1.5	0
10% and above but less than 20%	10	Above 1.5	10
More than 20%	20	**Gearing (total debt/(total debt plus equity))**	
Interest cover		Less than 25%	20
No cover	–30	25% and above but less than 50%	10
Less than 1	–20	More than 50% less than 65%	0
More than 1 but less than 2	–10	Between 65% and 75%	–20
More than 2 but less than 4	0	Between 75% and 80%	–40
More than 4	10	Above 80%	–100

Risk	Aggregate score
Very low risk	Between 60 and 21
Low risk	Between 20 and 1
Medium risk	Between 0 and –24
High risk	Between –25 and –50
Very high risk	Above –50

The sales department has asked for a credit limit of £50,000 to be given to Cow Limited who is a potential new customer. The financial information below has been supplied by Cow Limited

Accounts for Cow Limited	20X1	20X2
Statement of profit or loss	£000	£000
Revenue	4,500	5,500
Cost of sales	3,500	3,800
Gross profit	1,000	1,700
Distribution costs	1,050	1,150
Administration costs	1,000	1,000
Operating profit	−1,050	−450
Finance cost	100	50
Profit before taxation	−1,150	−500
Tax	0	0
Profit for the year	−1,150	−500

Statement of financial position	20X1	20X2
	£000	£000
Non-current assets		
Tangible assets	2,200	2,500
Current assets		
Inventory	900	750
Trade receivables	1,000	850
Cash and cash equivalents	50	400
	1,950	2,000
Total assets	4,150	4,500
Equity		
Share capital	200	1,350
Retained earnings	850	850
	1,050	2,200
Non-current liabilities		
Loan	1,000	500
Current liabilities		
Trade payables	2,100	1,800
Total equity and liabilities	4,150	4,500

(a) Complete the table below by calculating the indicators (to 2 decimal places) and the credit rating for 20X1 and 20X2 for Cow Limited

Cow Limited	Indicator	Rating	Indicator	Rating
Year	20X1		20X2	
Operating profit margin %				
Interest cover				
Current ratio				
Gearing %				

Rating	Decision
Very low or low risk current year and very low risk or low risk previous year	Accept
Very low or low risk current year and medium risk previous year	Accept
Very low or low risk current year and high or very high risk previous year	Request latest management accounts and defer decision
Very high risk or high risk current year	Reject
Medium risk current year and medium, low or very low risk previous year	Accept
Medium risk current year and high or very high risk previous year	Request latest management accounts and defer decision

(b) Based on the results of your credit rating and using the table above the request for credit by Cow Ltd should be:

A Accepted

B Rejected

C Request latest management accounts and defer decision

Task 4

The sales department has asked for a credit limit of £30,000 to be given to Pig Limited who is a potential new customer. The financial information below has been supplied by Pig Limited. The sales department have stated that the inventory levels are high due to the seasonality of the business.

Accounts for Pig Limited	20X1	20X2
Statement of profit or loss	£000	£000
Revenue	8,000	9,000
Cost of sales	6,000	6,250
Gross profit	2,000	2,750
Distribution costs	850	850
Administration costs	600	600
Operating profit	550	1,300
Finance cost	250	250
Profit before taxation	300	1,050
Tax	100	350
Profit for the year	200	700

Statement of financial position	20X1	20X2
	£000	£000
Non-current assets		
Property, Plant and equipment	3,900	4,500
Current assets		
Inventory	1,000	1,200
Trade receivables	600	700
Cash and cash equivalents	400	400
	2,000	2,300
Total assets	**5,900**	**6,800**
Equity		
Share capital	100	100
Retained earnings	2,000	2,700
	2,100	2,800
Non-current liabilities		
Loan	2,500	2,500
Current liabilities		
Trade payables	1,300	1,500
Total equity and liabilities	**5,900**	**6,800**

(a) Complete the table below by calculating the indicators (to 2 decimal places) for 20X1 and 20X2 for Pig Limited

Pig Limited	Indicator	Indicator
Year	**20X1**	**20X2**
Operating profit margin %		
Gross profit margin %		
Current ratio		
Payable days		
Inventory days		

(b)   Complete the email to the chief credit controller commenting on the ratios calculated in (a) above and conclude by recommending whether or not credit should be extended. *** delete the wrong answers.**

Email

To: Credit controller   Date: Today

From: AAT Technician   Subject: New Customer Pig Limited

Please find below my observations and recommendations for new customer Pig Limited.

Profitability

The revenue has increase by ⬚ % which means that the company has *either sold more units or increased the price of its product/increased sales which means the company is overtrading/cut its price to increase demand**. The most important indicator for profitability is the *operating profit margin/gross profit margin/current ratio** which has increased by **109.88%/52.35%/22.24%/18.19%***. *This is a good sign/This is a bad sign**

The gross profit margin has improved from 20X1 to 20X2 which is a good sign/The operating profit margin has improved from 20X1 to 20X2 which is a good sign*. This shows the profit after the costs of manufacture have been charged but before the distribution and administration costs have been charged.

Liquidity

The current ratio provides *an approximate measure of the short term liquidity of the business/a measure of long term liquidity**.

In this case it has fallen marginally but is *still greater than 1 which is a good sign/less than 1 which is a sign of insolvency/greater than 1 which is not a good sign as the current ratio should always be less than 1**.

The inventory holding period has *decreased/increased**.

This appears to be a strong sign of overtrading/This is a concern because when revenue grows inventory levels should reduce/This appears to be fine because as the business grows the inventory levels normally grow*.

The trade payables payment period in days has *increased/decreased**

We cannot give credit as our terms are 30 days so we will not be paid to terms/This can probably be explained by the high inventory levels caused by the seasonality of the business/This is a cause for concern especially as our terms of trade are 30 days and we should only give credit with a bank guarantee*.

I recommend that the *credit be granted/credit not be granted**

Task 5

Chicken Limited has been trading with Lamb Limited for several years and has, until recently, always paid to terms. Following several late payments they have now contacted Lamb Limited to request an increase in their credit limit from £50,000 to £100,000. Chicken Limited has supplied the accounts below.

Accounts for Chicken Limited	20X1	20X2
Statement of profit or loss	£000	£000
Revenue	6,000	6,500
Cost of sales	3,800	4,600
Gross profit	2,200	1,900
Distribution costs	850	850
Administration costs	600	600
Operating profit	750	450
Finance cost	250	500
Profit before taxation	500	–50
Tax	150	0
Profit for the year	350	–50

Statement of financial position	20X1	20X2
	£000	£000
Non-current assets		
Property, plant and equipment	4,350	7,050
Current assets		
Inventory	550	1,200
Trade Receivables	800	1,300
Cash and cash equivalents	300	100
	1,650	2,600
Total assets	**6,000**	**9,650**
Equity		
Share capital	100	100
Retained earnings	2,500	2,450
	2,600	2,550

Non-current liabilities		
Long term loans	2,000	5,000
Current liabilities		
Trade payables	1,400	2,100
Total equity and liabilities	**6,000**	**9,650**

Additional information supplied by the sales department after a visit to Chicken Limited:

Chicken Limited has recently acquired several new large customers and therefore purchased new assets with long term loans to ensure that forecast sales demands can be met. The contracts with the new customers were only completed in the second half of the year, and it is expected that sales will continue to increase in 20X2 with little increase in costs because the new machines have resulted in a reduction in variable cost per unit. The directors of Chicken Limited expect a profit after tax in 20X3 of around £500,000. In anticipation of orders for 20X3, Chicken Limited significantly increased its inventory levels at the end of 20X2.

Chicken Limited	Indicator	Indicator
Year	**20X1**	**20X2**
Operating profit margin %	12.5	6.92
Interest cover	3.00	0.90
Current ratio	1.18	1.24
Trade payable payment period in days	134.47	166.63
Trade receivables collection period in days	48.67	73.00
Inventory holding period in days	52.83	95.22
Gearing %	43.48	66.23

(a)   Write a brief note to explain whether Chicken Limited is overtrading by stating the signs of overtrading and considering Chicken Limited's indicators (use additional paper if required).

(b)   Write a report considering all the information and decide whether Chicken Limited should be given extended credit terms

Please note that there is not one correct answer to this task as any assessment is subjective. You need to justify your decision based on a range of indicators. You can make use of addition terms in the contract or any other options open to Lamb Limited which could provide additional comfort (use additional paper if required).

Task 6

You have been provided with the credit control policy for Lamb Limited and an aged receivable's analysis at 31 March 20X2.

Credit control policy for Lamb Limited.

Current credit control procedures once credit limit has been agreed:

1   An order for goods is received by email, fax or phone (all phone calls are recorded).

2   Goods are delivered and a goods received note is signed by the customer.

3   The goods received notes are kept in a file in the accounts office.

4   An invoice will be issued a few days after delivery on 30 day terms.

5   An aged analysis of trade receivables is produced monthly.

6   A reminder telephone call is made when the debt is 7 days overdue.

7   When a debt is 14 days overdue a letter is sent.

8   When the account is 28 days overdue the account will be put on stop.

9   The debt will either be placed in the hands of a debt collection company or legal proceedings could be instigated if the customer does not respond to calls or letters.

10   The business is credit insured, however insurance is only given for customers once they have a history of trade with the business of at least 12 months and have successfully paid for at least 3 invoiced amounts.

Aged receivables analysis as at 31 March 20X2

Customer	Balance £	0 – 30 days £	31 – 60 days £	61 – 90 days £	Over 90 days £
Pink	10,000	10,000			
Blue	25,000			25,000	
Green	60,000	30,000	30,000		
White	35,000	10,000	10,000	15,000	
Brown	60,000	60,000			
Cerise	25,000	5,000	20,000		

The assistant responsible for credit control has been on sick leave for several months but you have access to notes she prepared.

Notes provided by the assistant credit controller

A   Pink is a new customer and placed its first order a few weeks ago.

B   Blue have said that they placed an order for a particular grade of product but received a different product and are therefore not prepared to pay the invoice.

C   Green is a new customer and has said that a cheque is in the post. There is a rumour circulating that the company is having financial problems and has not been paying its suppliers. Green has placed an order for £10,000 of goods.

D   White has a history of paying late but they have always paid eventually.

E   Brown is a long standing customer and has always settled their account within trading terms.

F   Cerise has gone into administration. The account is not credit insured.

Complete the table below by selecting from the following list of options:

- A chasing letter should be sent and the account should be on stop. A telephone call maybe needed to discuss credit terms.

- Put the account on stop until payment is received, do not process any more orders. A provision for the outstanding amounts may be provided for.

- Contact the insolvency practitioner to register a claim and a provision should be made in the accounts.

- Check the sales order and delivery note for any error.

- No action needed.

Customer	Action
Pink	
Blue	
Green	
White	
Brown	
Cerise	

Task 7

You have been provided with the credit control policy for Lamb Limited and an aged receivable's analysis at 31 March 20X2.

Credit control policy for Lamb Limited.

Current credit control procedures once credit limit has been agreed:

1   An order for goods is received by email, fax or phone (all phone calls are recorded).

2   Goods are delivered and a goods received note is signed by the customer.

3   The goods received notes are kept in a file in the accounts office.

4   An invoice will be issued a few days after delivery on 30 day terms.

5   An aged analysis of trade receivables is produced monthly.

6   A reminder telephone call is made when the debt is 7 days overdue.

7   When a debt is 14 days overdue a letter is sent.

8   When the account is 28 days overdue the account will be put on stop.

9   The debt will either be placed in the hands of a debt collection company or legal proceedings could be instigated if the customer does not respond to calls or letters.

10 The business is credit insured, however insurance is only given for customers once they have a history of trade with the business of at least 12 months and have successfully paid for at least 3 invoiced amounts.

Aged receivables analysis as at 31 March 20X2

Customer	Balance £	0 – 30 days £	31 – 60 days £	61 – 90 days £	Over 90 days £
Red	10,000	(50,000)	10,000		50,000
Yellow	25,000				25,000
Violet	33,000	33,000			
Amber	20,000			20,000	
Mauve	120,000	30,000	30,000	30,000	30,000
Beige	40,000	20,000	20,000		
Taupe	99,200		44,200	55,000	
Auburn	100,000			100,000	

Notes provided by the assistant credit controller

A   Red sent a payment of £50,000 but did not provide details of which invoices the payment relates to.

B   Yellow is a new customer and has said that the goods were not received in good condition. The delivery note states that any claim for poor quality goods has to be notified to Lamb Limited within 24 hours. Yellow only raised a problem with the goods when they were called for the second time. They did not mention that the goods were poor quality on the first call or within 24 hours of delivery.

C   Violet is a new customer and has only placed the one order. They have not responded to any correspondence and the letter was returned stating the company had gone away.

D   Amber is a new business and traded on cash with order. The assistant credit controller allowed the order to be processed before the cheque had cleared. The cheque subsequently bounced and the company is not returning calls.

E   Mauve is a long established customer and has always paid eventually, but has a history of late payments. The Managing Director of Mauve is a personal friend of Lamb Limited's Managing Director.

F   Beige has been purchasing £20,000 per month.

G   Taupe is a regular customer and normally pays but payment can take several months – usually once a notice of intention to start legal proceedings in issued.

H   Auburn has recently gone into liquidation. Auburn had been a customer for 5 years and the account is credit insured.

Review the aged trade receivables analysis and the assistant's notes and prepare an action plan. The action plan should include a summary of options available for the company to pursue and recommendations for provisions or write off of irrecoverable debts where appropriate.

2 Mock Assessment Answers

Task 1

(a) **B** Offer, acceptance, consideration, intention to create legal relations and certainty of terms only

(b) **D** Promising to pay for the takeaway

(c) **D** An invitation to treat

(d) **B** Mark's letter is an offer and John's response that he can supply the sugar is an acceptance

(e) **B** An action for price

(f) **C** The right of the seller to retain ownership of the goods until payment is made

(g) **A** There is a contract in existence and the non payment is a breach of contract

(h) £168.66

£6,000 × 1.2 × 9.5% × 90 ÷ 365

(i) **A** Data about individuals only

Task 2

(a) **D** Liquidity management is important so that the company can ensure that cash is available to discharge commitments

(b) **B** £750

(c) **B** (i), (ii) and (iii) only

(d) **C** 101.39%

(e) **A** Amounts owed by a customer who has defaulted on payment

(f) **D** Debt collection agencies get results because customers take more notice and are more likely to pay

(g) **C** Small claims track

(h) 21.57 days

£2,600 ÷ (5,500 × £8) × 365

(i) Ben can borrow £43,200. This is an example of (c) invoice discounting

Task 3

Cow Limited	Indicator	Rating	Indicator	Rating
Year	20X1		20X2	
Operating profit margin %	−23.33	−5	−8.18	−5
Interest cover	0	−30	0	−30
Current ratio	0.92	−20	1.11	−10
Gearing %	48.78	10	18.52	20
		−45		−25

(b) Based on the results of your credit rating and using the table above the request for credit by Cow Limited should be:

B Rejected

Task 4

Pig Limited	Indicator	Indicator
Year	20X1	20X2
Operating profit margin %	6.88	14.44
Gross profit margin %	25.00	30.56
Current ratio	1.54	1.53
Payable days	79.08	87.60
Inventory days	60.83	70.08

(b)

Email

To: Credit controller   Date: Today

From: AAT Technician   Subject: New Customer Pig Limited

Please find below my observations and recommendations for new customer Pig Limited.

Profitability

The revenue has increase by **12.5**% which means that the company has *either sold more units or increased the price of its product.* The most important indicator for profitability is the *operating profit margin* which has increased by *109.88. This is a good sign.*

The gross profit margin has improved from 20X1 to 20X2 which is a good sign. This shows the profit after the costs of manufacture have been charged but before the distribution and administration costs have been charged.

Liquidity

The current ratio provides *an approximate measure of the short term liquidity of the business.*

In this case it has fallen marginally but is *still greater than 1 which is a good sign.*

The inventory holding period has *increased.*

This appears to be fine because as the business grows the inventory levels normally grow.

The trade payables payment period in days has *increased.*

This can probably be explained by the high inventory levels caused by the seasonality of the business.

I recommend that the *credit be granted.*

Task 5

Chicken Limited

(a) Write a brief note to explain whether Chicken Limited is overtrading by stating the signs of overtrading and considering Chicken Limited's indicators (use additional paper if required).

The signs of overtrading are as follows:

- Rapidly increasing sales revenue normally linked to extended credit terms.
- Reduced gross and operating margins.
- Increased inventory and trade receivables days.
- Reduction in cash or an increase in overdraft.
- Increased trade payable days.

Chicken Limited's performance indicators:

- Revenue has increased by 8%.
- Operating profit margin has declined.
- Gross profit margin has also declined (20X1 = 37% and 20X2 = 29%).
- Inventory levels have more than doubled from X1 to X2 and the holding period has increased by 42 days.
- Trade receivables have increased by 63% from X1 to X2 and the collection period has increased by about 24 days.
- Cash has reduced but is still positive.
- Trade payables have increased by 50% and the payment period has increased by 33 days.

It is possible that Chicken Limited was overtrading.

(b) Write a report considering all the information and decide whether Chicken Limited should be given extended credit terms

Please note that there is not one correct answer to this task as any assessment is subjective. You need to justify your decision based on a range of indicators. You can make use of addition terms in the contract or any other options open to Lamb Limited which could provide additional comfort (use additional paper if required).

Profitability

The revenue has grown but the profitability has declined,

Interest cover has fallen significantly,

These are both warning signs but the company has recently purchased new assets using a long term loan. This could be the explanation.

Liquidity

The current ratio has improved but this is explained by the increase in receivables and inventory rather than cash. Receivables and inventory are less liquid than cash.

Trade payables have also increased but this may be distorted by the purchase of inventory to meet increased orders.

Debt (Borrowing)

Gearing has significantly increased but this is due to the loan taken out to purchase the new machinery.

There is no overdraft in use.

The bank has provided this company with a loan which is a good sign. It may be necessary to check how much security the company has offered the bank to secure this loan.

Summary

There are some worrying indicators for Chicken Limited and it would appear that Chicken Limited is now higher risk than it was previously.

A meeting could be set up with the company to discuss the extension of the credit limit to see more up to date accounts.

If the more current accounts show that the anticipated orders are coming in then the extension could be considered.

Chicken Limited is still liquid with cash in the bank at the year end

There are certain factors in its favour. These include:

- A good trading history over several years, although recently they have made some late payments.

- The expansion plan and the fact that the bank has given loans for the purchase of new assets is a good sign.

- New customers have ordered goods and have indicated that they will continue in 2013.

- The company is still liquid with cash at bank at the year end.

It is worth considering taking some kind of security over the business or personal guarantees from the directors or to consider retention of title clauses. There is no right decision and as long as the credit controller considers all the issues and makes a reasoned decision, credit will be awarded.

Task 6

Customer	Action
Pink	No action needed.
Blue	Check the sales order and delivery note for any error.
Green	Put the account on stop until payment is received, do not process any more orders. A provision for the outstanding amounts may be provided for.
White	A chasing letter should be sent and the account should be on stop. A telephone call maybe needed to discuss credit terms.
Brown	No action needed.
Cerise	Contact the insolvency practitioner to register a claim and a provision should be made in the accounts.

Task 7

Red

A telephone call is needed to confirm which invoice the payment is against.

Yellow

Under the terms and conditions any fault should have been notified to Lamb Limited within 24 hours of receipt. The account should be placed on stop and Yellow should be notified that legal proceeding will be started if payment is not received. A provision for the debt should be made.

Violet

A telephone call is required to check postal details. A provision for the debt should be provided as there is uncertainty.

Amber

Lamb Limited needs to investigate how this could happen. The credit controller responsible for this needs to been spoken to. Telephone calls need to be made to locate Amber and chase for payment. Legal proceedings may be started if necessary. A provision should be provided at this stage, a write off may be necessary.

Mauve

Lamb Limited's MD should have a chat with Mauve's MD as usual credit control lines have not succeeded. Account may be put on stop until this conversation has been had.

Beige

Beige is already at its credit limit so no more orders should be processed until the payment is received.

Taupe

The account should be put on stop and credit terms revised.

Auburn

The insurance company should be contacted to regain the debt.

INDEX

KAPLAN PUBLISHING